An Introduction to Pike Fishing

An Introduction to Pike Fishing

David Batten

The Crowood Press

First published in 1989 by
The Crowood Press Ltd
Ramsbury, Marlborough
Wiltshire, SN8 2HR

Paperback edition 1994

British Library Cataloguing-in-Publication Data

A catalogue record of this book is
available from the British Library

ISBN 1 85223 823 2

Acknowledgements

Photographs by the author, Colin Brett and Chris Turnbull
Line-drawings by the author.

Typeset by PCS Typesetting, Frome, Somerset
Printed and bound in Great Britain by
BPC Hazell Books Ltd
A member of
The British Printing Company Ltd

Contents

Introduction

Choosing to pick up a book on pike fishing is a very important move and undoubtedly you will not regret the effort. This book in particular is designed to help both established and prospective pike anglers. It will certainly help you consolidate an approach that will give you a confident and consistent result in the catching of pike. Many books have been written about pike fishing; all have a great deal to offer, but only a few cover what the newcomer to pike fishing needs to know. Here, the newcomer and the experienced pike angler will find some of the answers to questions as yet unexplained.

There has recently been a surge of interest in pike fishing, due mainly to the fact that it is a species, like carp and catfish, that grows to in excess of thirty pounds. This generates a desire in an angler to catch such a fish, which is further fuelled by the regular appearances, in weekly and monthly publications, of anglers who have succeeded in catching such specimens – indeed some who have caught even bigger fish!

Along with this increased interest, there has been a leap forward in tackle technology which has caused numerous misunderstandings, as it has failed to explain to the angler exactly how to use the new tackle. Hopefully, through the chapters of this book, some of the misunderstandings will be explained and as a result more pike will fall to *confident, caring,* anglers.

The purpose of this book is to help build a *confident* approach to playing, landing and more importantly *handling* the pike you catch. Too long has the pike been forced to suffer at the hands of unsure anglers, who fail to take control of the very situation in which they hoped to find themselves. With a pike of moderate proportions, or maybe even the angler's and water's best, enmeshed in a landing net awaiting unhooking, it would be such a shame to risk killing or badly injuring it. After all, you would not wound or kill the loser in any other sport.

Perhaps this book is a plea for more caring treatment of the pike, as it is unable to speak for itself. It has been written and illustrated with consideration for both angler and prey.

1 Pike – The Species

Few anglers who intend fishing for pike will be totally ignorant about the fish, but many may lack some understanding about some of the more important facts relating to the fish, its role in nature and its value to a fishery. This chapter will hopefully provide some basic background information, which will help you to understand the pike and how it functions. It is not intended to be an in-depth study, but more a brief outline.

CHARACTERISTICS

The fish we are concerned with, *Esox lucius*, is immediately recognisable, unlike some of the cyprinoid species. It has a long, streamlined body with a large tail, and rearward set anal and dorsal fins which allow strong, rapid acceleration to catch its prey. The large, tooth-filled mouth is designed to deal easily with live, very slippery prey – and to cast fear into those who unwittingly catch a pike by

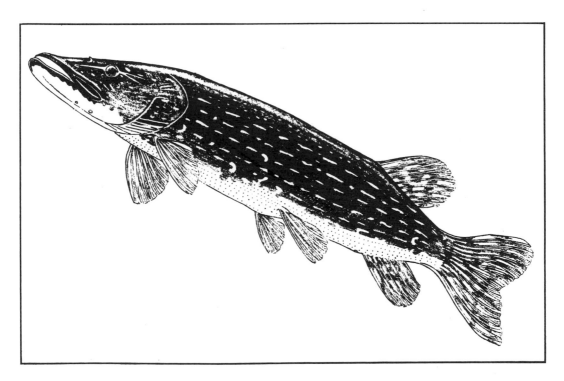

Fig 1 Body markings – full fish.

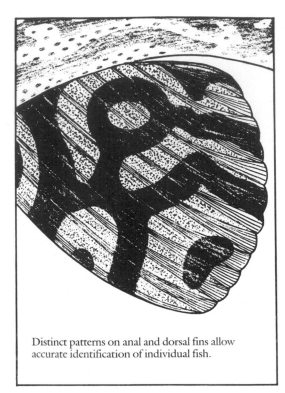

Distinct patterns on anal and dorsal fins allow accurate identification of individual fish.

Fig 2   Anal fin markings.

mistake. The mottled effect, covering the body with deep greens and browns (depending on its environment), fading down the flanks to a creamy, almost white belly, supplies the fish with camouflage, so that it can conceal itself from its prey in weed and reed beds until able to strike effectively. The mottling effect changes through the early years when bar markings, noticeable on very young fish, change to more broken patches covering the whole body. These markings become very distinctive in later years and, along with the similar markings on the fins, allow accurate identification of individual fish – as accurate as human fingerprints in fact.

Some of these marks are like the letter 'C', or a reverse letter 'C' (*see* Fig 1); some fin markings are like bullseyes (*see* Fig 2). Markings on some fish encountered are directly related to the environment in which they live. For example, fish from the clear waters of reservoirs tend to have a pattern of markings like those of the light reflections seen on the bottom in shallow water.

Senses

With its eyes positioned high on its head, the pike is particularly successful as a predator. Its eye position gives it binocular-type vision forwards so that it can judge exactly the distance to its prey when striking to kill. They also allow good upward vision – an important point to remember when you are presenting a bait. If the pike is lying stationary on the bottom amongst weed, a bait passing over its head is more likely to be investigated than a static bait lying on the bottom some distance away. In certain environments, deadbaits are located shortly after casting, as they fall from above, possibly by sight or through the pressure on the pike's lateral line caused by the splash of the bait's impact. It is likely that the pike is alerted by the lateral line, and effects a visual sighting as a result.

Undoubtedly, the second most important sense is that of smell. The pike's olfactory organs are located just forward of the eyes, at the top of the slope up from the jaw and mouth, allowing any scent in the water from a food source to pass over them whilst the pike is moving forward. It is important to note that the pike is very capable of locating deadbaits in coloured water. This again should be remembered and capitalised on when the waters you are fishing are heavily coloured. You should use fresh deadbaits and even introduce an extra scent or flavour to them, to give the fish something greater to home in on. Livebaits may be located by vibration through the lateral line, but smells travel

A beautifully marked pike from the crystal clear waters of a reservoir.

further in the water, giving the pike a greater location range.

Shape

Different environments will alter the pike's shape and length. Fish from old, established lakes with low volumes of prey fish are usually long and lean. Pike from reservoirs that are high in prey fish are very much the opposite, being short and very plump, particularly if they are taken from trout-stocked waters! The heads on these fish also appear small, but this would seem to be relative to their age. Short, plump fish are usually very young, and they have great potential for growing into very big fish indeed. Fish found in the Norfolk Broads, and other areas where the predominant feed fish are bream, have long bodies and larger heads and mouths, to cope with their larger-bodied prey.

Weight

By measuring the weight of recaptured known fish, it has been shown that annual increases in weight can vary from one to three pounds, but usually average one and a half to two pounds. This, however, does not take into account the spawning period, when a further two to five pounds of weight might be carried depending on the fish's normal size. The female of the species is the bigger; the male fish rarely, if ever, exceeds ten pounds. Mature males of seven to nine pounds are often caught, but no noticeable increase in weight year to year has been noted in recaptured male fish.

Spawning usually takes place during March and April each year, but this is very much dependent on the prevailing weather conditions and the water temperatures. Once the temperature of the water starts to rise above 40°F (5°C), the urge to spawn brings pike to congregate on their regular spawning sites. Usually the males appear in quantity first, followed by the females. In many fisheries these activities are heralded by large catches of small- to medium-sized pike, of five to seven pounds in weight. These will usually be all male, but if you are lucky and are in the right place when this activity commences you might be fortunate enough to contact some of the large females when they finally move in as well. Some phenomenal catches have taken place on waters when anglers have located, usually by chance, just such an aggregation of pike.

2 Baits

Your choice of baits will depend on the methods you use and the waters you fish. If you are faced with preoccupied, fry-feeding pike, you may decide to use livebaits; or you may come across a coloured, shallow water and find that deadbaits make a more viable option. With livebaits, you must either catch them in advance or on the day – and whichever way you choose to handle that situation, you would be well advised to take along a supply of deadbaits as an alternative, or as a back-up in case no livebait is available. Alternatively, you may wish not to use livebait at all but opt for using deadbaits and lures for all your piking.

VARIATION

Your choice of baits, and particularly deadbaits, could not be greater – walk into a good tackle dealer and you will usually find a freezer stocked to overflowing with a huge array of different baits. A few years ago, the selection was limited to herrings, mackerel and sprats, until a revolutionary bait came on the scene: the smelt. These could not be bought from fishmongers as they had no commercial value. They originally came from power station outfalls on rivers like the Thames, and were a chance find for anglers searching for sprats – what a find! Their apparent mystical power has been attributed to their cucumber-type smell, but, in fact, their real attraction was simply that they were different! On waters that had been heavily fished with mackerel, herring and sprat, the introduction of a new bait with a different smell was accepted as *safe* by the pike.

The subsequent reaction to the success of those anglers who started using smelt sparked off a revolution in the tackle trade. After Neville Flickling's claims that his record pike of 41lb 6oz fell to the humble smelt as bait, demand for them was phenomenal. Suddenly there was a commercial demand for them, so a few trawler skippers were now able to find a market for what had previously been a nuisance and a time-waster.

With time, the variety has increased to a point where any small sea-fish is likely to be of use. The current range of baits includes mackerel, herring, smelt, sardines, sandeels, horse mackerel, eels and sprats. The need to find alternatives has also generated a market for small dead trout, which, due to genetic defects from mass forced artificial spawning, were unsaleable to trout fisheries. In the past they have been processed for animal feed or just dumped; now there is a market for these and any excess production of normal fish. This has again benefited the deadbaiting pike angler by supplying yet another new bait.

The message to be remembered here is that whatever you do, make an effort to be different. If everybody is using one or two particular types of deadbait, you should try something else. With the wide variety available today you should be able to ring the changes from water to water and increase your opportunities of getting a take.

Flavourings

If everybody is using the full range of baits, or you cannot get hold of any of these alternatives, do not despair. There is another option which will allow you to achieve a similar effect, as it is possible to change the flavour, smell and colour of your bait or even all three. Simply go along to your tackle dealer, check out the carp bait flavouring stocks, and sort out some suitable flavourings and oils. The savoury or fishy ones will be the first to try, but anything can work – remember the cucumber smell of the smelt? What you will be doing is giving your bait a different *label* which for a short time will fool the pike in a given water. Some specific pike attractors are now marketed and are very useful.

There are two ways of getting the flavouring into the bait, with varying effects. The first is to soak a piece of cotton wool with the chosen flavour or oil and then push this into the mouth and throat of the bait. The second is to use a hypodermic syringe to inject the flavour or oil into the body cavity or flesh of the bait. These will slowly leach out of the bait acting as an attractor (*see* Fig 3).

Colourings

Using artificial colouring is also an alternative to changing baits. The easiest way is to immerse the bait in a cold water dye such as 'Dylon', although some of the newer carp bait

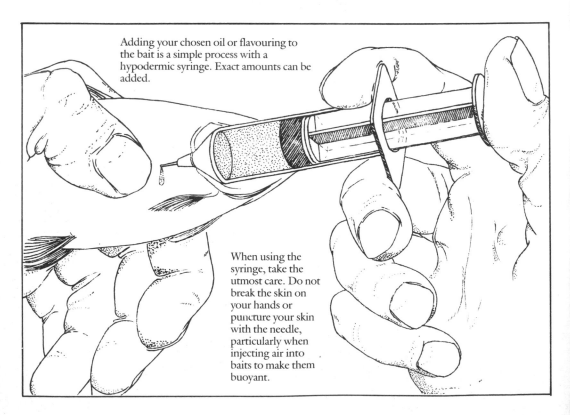

Adding your chosen oil or flavouring to the bait is a simple process with a hypodermic syringe. Exact amounts can be added.

When using the syringe, take the utmost care. Do not break the skin on your hands or puncture your skin with the needle, particularly when injecting air into baits to make them buoyant.

Fig 3   Injecting flavourings or oils.

Baits positioned and the adrenaline flows as the wait begins, beside the hot spot.

Chris Turnbull with 22lb 2oz Norfolk pike taken on buoyant horse mackerel (scad).

colourings may work, particularly the new permanent type that is not supposed to fade.

If you are using 'Dylon', dissolve the dye in cold water and immerse the bait fully, leaving it in long enough to absorb adequate colour. If the colour does not take too well into the scales, you may well have to scrape them off, as the colour is absorbed more easily into the skin tissue, particularly with sea-fish baits. The colouring of coarse fish deadbaits can be effected in the same way – although the mucus slime covering the body will absorb the colour more readily, so scale removal may not be necessary. Experiment with yellows, oranges and reds. When the dyeing is complete make sure you rinse off all the excess with cold water.

In addition to using flavouring and colouring individually, you can try combinations of different flavours and colours together and perhaps find a particularly useful attractive bait. But remember, any *different* bait might put those extra pike on the bank when all else has failed.

BUOYANT BAITS

There is another way to improve the attractiveness of deadbaits and that is to change their characteristics and presentation. Sea-fish deadbaits can be made buoyant, whilst coarse fish deadbaits can be given improved buoyancy. To do this you can use air, injected

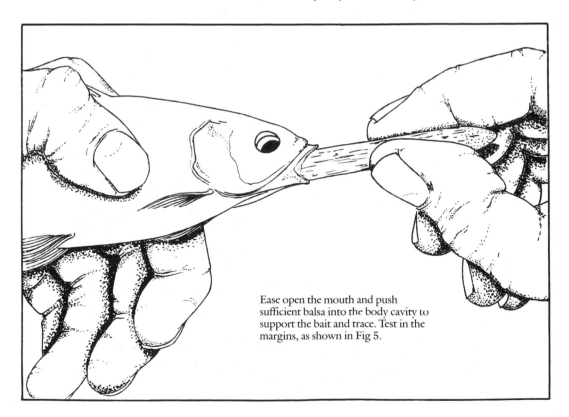

Ease open the mouth and push sufficient balsa into the body cavity to support the bait and trace. Test in the margins, as shown in Fig 5.

Fig 4   Inserting oil-soaked balsa into body cavity.

bait should be visible above silt and weed and move enticingly in the current or under tow.

Fig 5   Buoyant bait.

into the body with a hypodermic syringe, although this is unreliable, as the air gets knocked out on impact with the water after casting.

Balsa Inserts

A more effective way is to insert a piece of balsa wood into the body cavity. Balsa is likely to absorb water, so it will need waterproofing first. Seal the wood with a fish-based oil, such as pilchard oil or something similar. Soak it in warm or hot oil for a few minutes, and then place the treated sticks in a sealed polythene bag. The balsa spears should be tapered at either end, 2–4in long and ¼–⁵⁄₁₆in in diameter. To insert them into the bait, squeeze the mouth open and then push the stick down the throat and into the body cav-

ity, as shown in Fig 4. Then test the bait with the trace on, in the margins, until it becomes sufficiently buoyant.

Do not use chunks of polystyrene or sticks of balsa sealed in varnish to make your baits buoyant. Plain balsa can dissolve in the stomach acids of the pike as it is organic matter, but sealing in varnish stops this process. It also hardens the balsa, which may damage an internal organ if the balsa is pointed and sharp. It may also pierce the stomach lining. Polystyrene cannot dissolve, and the volume needed to make a large bait buoyant, may, if sufficient baits containing it are taken, make the internal balance of the pike unstable, with unpleasant consequences. It is far safer to use oil-sealed balsa inserts. Fig 5 shows the action of a buoyant bait.

Buoyant baits will be a great advantage

Drift-caught small-water double for the author.

A Fenland double taken on half mackerel for Mike Woods.

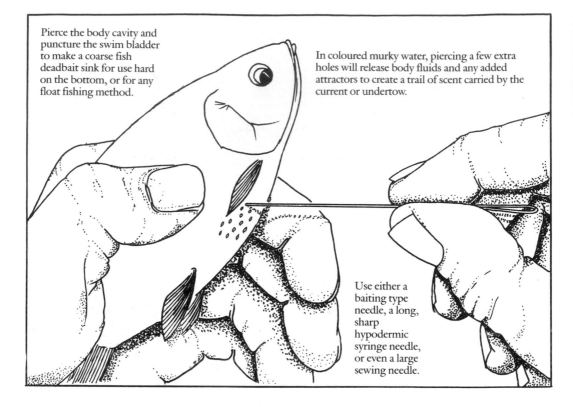

Pierce the body cavity and puncture the swim bladder to make a coarse fish deadbait sink for use hard on the bottom, or for any float fishing method.

In coloured murky water, piercing a few extra holes will release body fluids and any added attractors to create a trail of scent carried by the current or undertow.

Use either a baiting type needle, a long, sharp hypodermic syringe needle, or even a large sewing needle.

Fig 6   Piercing the swim bladder on coarse fish.

when fishing over soft silt or weed remnants. They also attract attention by being visible, off the bottom and moving around in the undertow and current.

The natural buoyancy of coarse fish can cause problems with float fished tactics. To overcome this you will need to pierce the body cavity with a sharp baiting-type needle (*see* Fig 6), making sure that you pierce the swim bladder. Again test the bait in the margins before casting (*see* Fig 8). This piercing will also release body fluids, or your added flavouring, to attract the pike. Non-buoyant baits may be necessary to get a response from the fish, as they have strange fancies on some days, so try buoyant *and* non-buoyant baits when necessary. The non-buoyant baits will

obviously work better over a clean lake bed.

Illustrated in Fig 7 are some various deadbait sizes, and the appropriate styles of traces that you might wish to use. The style you choose will be decided by the size and the type of bait available. The most critical factor in layout is that the trace should not be bigger than half the bait length – slightly shorter if possible, to prevent deep hooking when a bait is swallowed quickly. A variety of traces, ready-made and stored in a trace tidy, will make this task a lot easier.

Flavoured and coloured baits can be used together in both clear and cloudy water, but if you are not colouring you will find an added flavour may help pike to locate your bait in

For small baits of up to 2oz, use single size 6 or size 8 semi-barbless trebles.

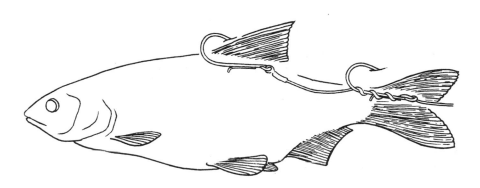

For medium-sized baits of 2–4oz use two size 8 VB double hooks or two size 6 or size 8 semi-barbless trebles.

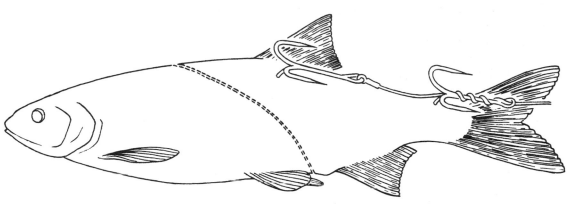

For large sectioned or whole baits of 4oz or more, use two size 6 or size 8 semi-barbless trebles or 2 size 6 VB double hooks.

Fig 7   Deadbait with sample trace mounts.

cloudy water. A combination of a coloured, suspended bait in clear water may be the ideal method. Whatever the conditions that seem to be affecting the response to your bait offering, try a combination or single application of these suggestions until you contact some fish. Do not be frightened to experiment if nothing happens, but do give the bait a reasonable chance. Ultimately, check you have correctly located the pike.

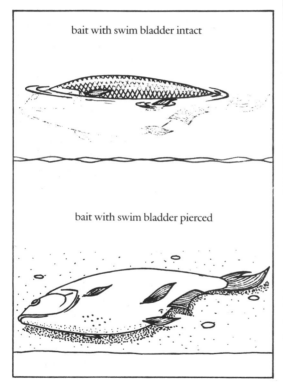

Fig 8   Non-buoyant coarse fish.

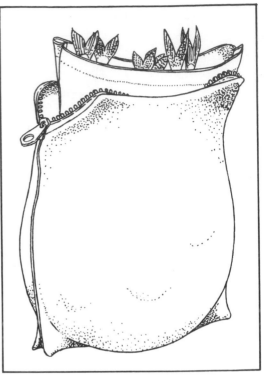

Fig 9   Boily bag with bait.

STORAGE

Many of today's baits are frozen and sealed in bags – this is what you should do with fresh bait which you may buy from the fishmonger. The best way is to individually wrap each bait in clingfilm before freezing. This will allow you to take only the amount you will need and not more, and also to carry a variety. Use a cool box or a chiller bag filled with freezer blocks to carry the bait – again you will find the ideal commodity in the carp tackle at your local dealer: a large boily bag! (*See* Fig 9.)

3 Tackle

Put ten capable pike anglers together on a new water and you will witness ten individual approaches to tackle. Eventually, one or more will find a method or item of tackle that makes the fishing on that water successful. The others will then copy and refine it to their own liking, so evolving new methods and items of tackle.

RODS

When you choose a rod for pike fishing, you should first consider just what you will require from your tackle, and the type of water you intend to fish. In the early days you will probably be considering fishing small waters, but if you then find you want to fish the really big waters, you will have to make a compromise initially – unless you have an extremely generous benefactor who can supply funds to purchase two of every rod available!

You must consider where you will fish most and what sort of fishing it will be. Short-range, long-range, deep water, shallow water, bank fishing and boat fishing will all ideally require their own type of rod. So you see, until you build up a full range of rods, there is a need for compromise in the rod you purchase.

The introduction of Kevlar reinforced carbon fibre is one of the greatest single innovations in pike fishing rods. These are now available in lengths up to thirteen feet, in test curves from 2 to 3 pounds in various taper actions, from full compound to fast taper.

There is a rod for every pike fisherman, from the short-range angler to the long-range casting and drifting angler, all of whom require something a little bit different from their rods. The other benefits of carbon fibre are lightness and diameter for size, and the positive feel the rods give when a fish is hooked and the hook is pulled home.

As a guideline, a suggested test curve would be 2 to 2½ pounds, with either a compound, through action or at least a medium taper action rod. This will allow live- and deadbaits to be cast easily at close and medium ranges and have sufficient power to set the hooks and control the pike once hooked. Too heavy a test curve and too steep a taper will limit you to long-range work and be pretty useless for short-range, soft bait work.

The cost of carbon fibre has remained stable for several years now and if you can afford them, buy rods or blanks made of this material. If, however, you are limited in the amount you have to spend, there are still some good, proven fibreglass rods and blanks available, which are listed in Fig 11. There are plenty of lower priced carbon-fibre rods on the market but, like everything else, you only get what you pay for. Many of these low cost carbons will lead to disappointment when they break whilst casting or when playing a big fish, as many anglers have found to their cost!

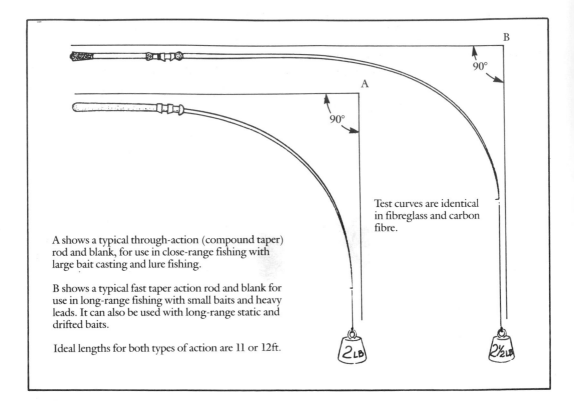

A shows a typical through-action (compound taper) rod and blank, for use in close-range fishing with large bait casting and lure fishing.

B shows a typical fast taper action rod and blank for use in long-range fishing with small baits and heavy leads. It can also be used with long-range static and drifted baits.

Ideal lengths for both types of action are 11 or 12ft.

Test curves are identical in fibreglass and carbon fibre.

Fig 10   Rod test curve and actions.

REELS

In keeping with the development in rods, the reel manufacturers have taken heed of what anglers want and top quality, purpose-built reels are now available. Most of these are of the fixed spool type, although some innovations in multiplier reel design have taken place, with ambidextrous models now being available from one manufacturer. However, these reels are of limited use by the average pike angler, as they are mainly used with lure and boat fishing, so it is probably best to stick to fixed spool models.

Your choice of reel is one governed by price and, again, you will get only what you are prepared to pay for. First choice of reel must fall with makes like Mitchell, with conventional models like the 300/300S/410 and, more recently, the rear drag, skirted spool 2250RD, a superb reel that will cover every kind of fishing, including pike. Another model, the 3350RD, has a full control lever which allows you to set the drag lower than necessary to enable a running fish to take line against the clutch, allowing you to then apply greater drag to slow the fish by applying the lever with your forefinger. You can then release the pressure to compensate should the fish make a last lunge for freedom when it sees the net – fine in principle, but expensive!

Other manufacturers who have produced fine reels include Shimano, with their Baitrunner range and its free spool mode which,

Manufacturer	Material	Model no. T/curve action
Tricast	Carbon/Aramid Fibre	12ft ER8–15 2¼lb fast taper
	Carbon/Aramid Fibre	12ft MU11–18 3lb compound taper
North Western	Carbon/Aramid Fibre	12ft CZ200 2lb compound taper
	Carbon/Aramid Fibre	12ft CZ275 2½lb fast taper
	Fibreglass	11ft SS5 2lb compound taper
	Fibreglass	11ft SS6 2½lb fast taper
	Fibreglass	11ft PK3 2¾lb fast taper

Fig 11   List of rods and blanks (carbon and fibreglass).

like the Mitchell 2250RD with a drag backed fully off, allows line to be taken with the bail arm 'closed'. The Baitrunner is great for boat fishing, as all that is needed to reset the drag is a turn of the handle. With the Mitchell, however, you have to reset the drag setting, *after* you have released the anti-reverse lever! As conventional reels, though, there is little to choose between them and both are recommended. If you cannot afford either, then look closely at the conventional Mitchell range, especially the Mitchell 300S skirted spool model.

Spool capacities are another important feature, as are spool materials. Many today are graphite composite spools (plastic-type) materials) and are prone to damage. Under certain circumstances they can actually break in two. This is usually caused by the compres-sing action of fully stretched monofilament line from playing a big fish, or trying to release a fish or bait from a snag, or simply playing a fish at extreme range. The old Mitchell alloy spools take some beating but hopefully reel manufacturers will master the problems of the new plastics as time passes.

LINE

To make the tackle balance correctly, the choice of line is also crucial. After all, it is the means of connecting you with your quarry. Get the balance wrong and you risk breakage on the cast, the strike or during the fight to land your fish. The type and strength of line you choose should be decided by the style of fishing and the appropriate tackle you will

Manufacturer	Line Type	Breaking Strain	Diameter
Maxima	Chameleon	12lb	0.013in
Maxima	Chameleon	15lb	0.015in
Sylcast	Sorrel	11lb	0.013in
Sylcast	Sorrel	15lb	0.014in
Drennan	Specimen Plus	12lb	0.013in

Fig 12   List of lines and breaking strains.

Paul Gribble proudly displays his Teach-In caught fish.

Another Teach-In caught fish and another confident junior returning it.

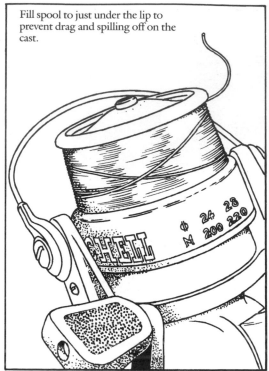

Fill spool to just under the lip to prevent drag and spilling off on the cast.

Fig 13   Correctly filled reel spool.

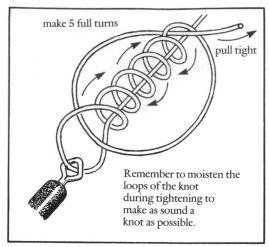

make 5 full turns

pull tight

Remember to moisten the loops of the knot during tightening to make as sound a knot as possible.

Fig 14   Blood knot (tucked).

use. Whilst many makes and types of line exist, some have a high degree of stretch and some are of low stretch. Both types have their applications and should be used accordingly. For 90 per cent of your pike fishing, the normal high-stretch line will be adequate. Typical examples are Maxima Chameleon and Sylcast Sorrel. Both of these have a sound pedigree and are used by a large proportion of today's pike anglers.

The breaking strain you would be well advised to use would be 11 pounds in Sylcast or 12 pounds in Maxima for normal conditions, and up to 15 pounds in both brands for snaggy waters, where the line might rub on an abrasive surface like branches, gravel bars or zebra mussels. Remember that the strength

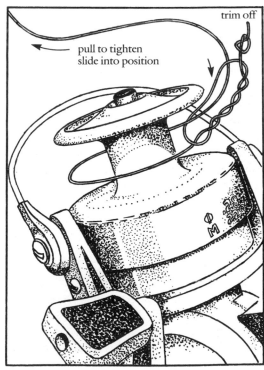

trim off

pull to tighten
slide into position

Fig 15   Spool tying knot.

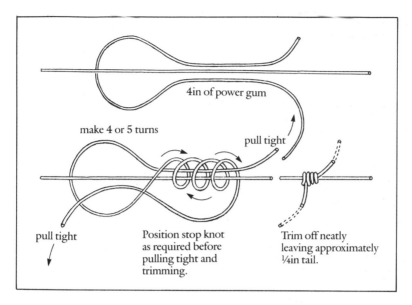

make 4 or 5 turns

4in of power gum

pull tight

pull tight

pull tight

Position stop knot as required before pulling tight and trimming.

Trim off neatly leaving approximately ¼in tail.

Fig 16   Stop knot (with power gum).

of your line must balance with your rod's test curve, so whilst you are recommended to use the strongest line, bear in mind that this will depend on the rod you choose to use. With our guideline of 2 to 2½-pound test curve medium action rods, 9 to 15-pound breaking strain line can be safely used. This balance is needed to allow you to safely cast large dead-baits, medium-sized livebaits, and anything up to two ounces of lead, smoothly without breakage of line or rod (*see* Figs 12 and 13).

An important point to remember with nylon monofilament line is that it will only be as strong as the weakest point, usually the knot. Some useful and practical varieties of knots appear in Figs 14, 15 and 16. Great care should be taken when tying all your knots, and all of them should be moistened to make them slide smoothly to the tightened position. Do not rush the tightening; take your time and you will get a stronger finish. Remember, it could make the difference between landing and losing that big pike.

ball-bearing swivel

Fig 17   Assorted swivels and links.

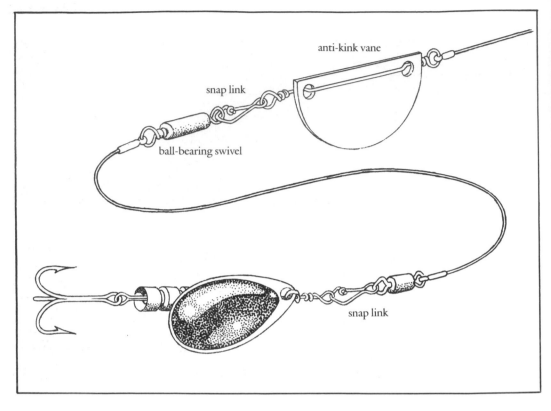

Fig 18   Anti-kink vane.

HOOKS, TRACES AND SWIVELS

Hooks, traces and swivels form the next most important part of the tackle, for it is these which will ensure that the bait is presented correctly. They also secure a hold on the pike and hopefully withstand its attempts to shed that hold and gain its freedom. Illustrated in Fig 17 are a variety of swivels and links which will stand up to the rigours of pike angling. The BB ball-bearing swivel is particularly recommended for spinning and general lure fishing in conjunction with an anti-kink vane, as shown in Fig 18. The diamond-shaped

Manufacturer	Type	Colour	Breaking Strain
PDQ	7 Strand Annealed	(Grey)	15lb and 20lb
Alasticum	7 Strand Annealed	(Grey)	15lb and 20lb
Marlin Steel	7 Strand Tempered Steel	(Light Green)	15lb and 20lb
Drennan Seven Strand	7 Strand Tempered Steel	(Brown)	15lb and 20lb
Pike Strand	7 Strand Tempered Steel	(Green)	15lb and 20lb

Fig 19   List of trace wires and breaking strains.

The golden back drop of Norfolk reeds around a Norfolk estate lake.

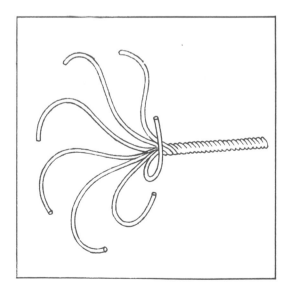

Fig 20   Layout of multi-strand wire.

swivels are particularly useful, as the trace and reel line sit neatly in the centre at all times. Various links to fit these swivels exist but the best is probably the Drennan Safe Loc, which will benefit from being covered in silicon tubing to stop the line or wire tangling with it at any time during the cast.

The wire used to make the traces is of great importance – it must be durable and supple with a fine diameter to allow good bait presentation, but it must also be very strong. All of this can only be achieved by using multi-strands of very fine wire twisted to make a cable-formed wire. Single-strand wire is too stiff and prone to kinking and breakage to be of any use. Fig 19 lists a variety of suitable trace wire makes and breaking strains. The breaking strain of the wire you use for your

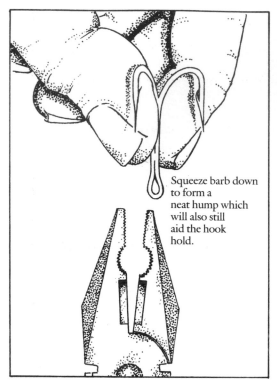

Squeeze barb down to form a neat hump which will also still aid the hook hold.

Fig 21   Squeezing down barbs.

traces should be 15 to 20 pounds, no less and no more, as all the wires on the market of this capacity will offer the required qualities.

Finally, to complete the trace, we come to the hooks. This is one area that will forever be a point of discussion between pike anglers, trying to decide on which make and pattern to use and whether they should be barbed or semi-barbless. As you progress as a pike angler you will undoubtedly make some definite decision on which hook you prefer. However, for the novice angler, semi-barbless hooks are recommended. You can buy them ready-made, or modify them yourself, by squeezing down with pliers or filing down to a small hump as shown in Fig 21. There are numerous types and patterns of hook available, from normal trebles, through special trebles to the recently introduced double hooks (*see* Fig 22). Many hooks are now available with extremely sharp, chemically etched points, making penetration much easier.

Manufacturer	Type	Pattern Number
Drennan	Carbon Semi-barbed Treble	–
Drennan	Semi-barbed Treble	–
Drennan	Special Carbon Treble (Barbed)	–
Drennan	Which Way Double Hooks (Barbed)	–
Partridge	Outpoint Semi-barbed Treble	W1
Partridge	Outpoint Barbed Carbon Steel Treble	CS9
Partridge	Outpoint Barbed Treble	X1
Partridge	VB Double Hooks (Barbed)	–
Mustad	Barb Trebles	3551
Mustad	Barb Trebles	35526
Mustad	Barb Trebles	35665
Ryobi	Eagle Claw Inturned Point Treble	–

Fig 22   List of hooks – doubles and trebles.

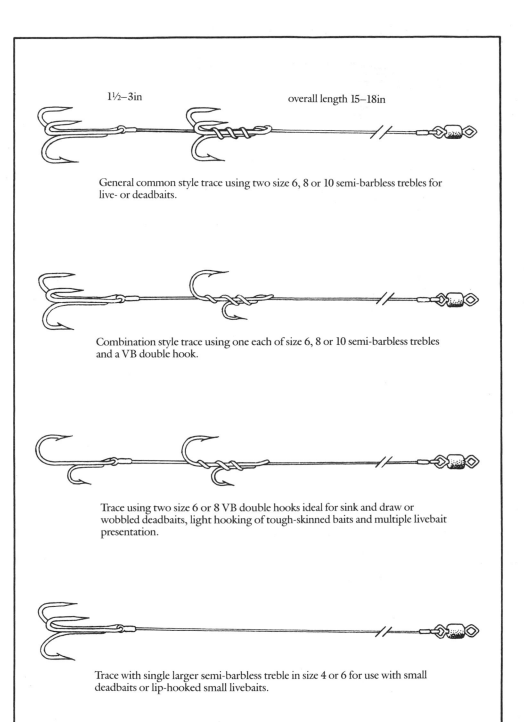

1½–3in   overall length 15–18in

General common style trace using two size 6, 8 or 10 semi-barbless trebles for live- or deadbaits.

Combination style trace using one each of size 6, 8 or 10 semi-barbless trebles and a VB double hook.

Trace using two size 6 or 8 VB double hooks ideal for sink and draw or wobbled deadbaits, light hooking of tough-skinned baits and multiple livebait presentation.

Trace with single larger semi-barbless treble in size 4 or 6 for use with small deadbaits or lip-hooked small livebaits.

Fig 23   A variety of trace types.

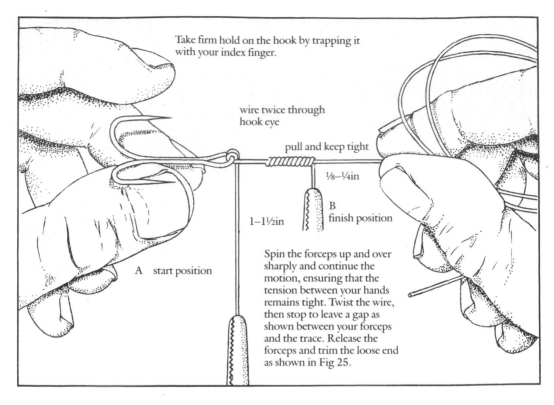

Take firm hold on the hook by trapping it with your index finger.

wire twice through hook eye

pull and keep tight

⅛–¼in

B finish position

1–1½in

A start position

Spin the forceps up and over sharply and continue the motion, ensuring that the tension between your hands remains tight. Twist the wire, then stop to leave a gap as shown between your forceps and the trace. Release the forceps and trim the loose end as shown in Fig 25.

Fig 24   Trace making: attaching and spinning the end hook.

SPINNING A TRACE

Trace lengths will vary to suit the conditions you will be confronted with, but a good basic working length would be fifteen to eighteen inches, giving good freedom of movement to livebaits and adequate length to prevent bite-offs. To get a trace of that length you will require a length of wire approximately four inches longer to allow for spinning.

Measure out eighteen to twenty inches of wire in the appropriate strength to suit the size of hooks and style of use you intend the trace for. Now, following the guideline illustrations in Fig 24, pass the wire through the first treble or double hook eye twice, leaving two inches of wire free to secure the trace. Now attach a pair of straight forceps and hold the hook and wire in preparation for spin-

ning. When ready, commence the spinning by virtually throwing the forceps up and away from you and continue the momentum by repeating this motion, keeping the rotating wire tight. Continue until nearly all the wire is wound round the tight wire you are holding. Before the forceps reach the same point, stop, leaving one-eighth to one-quarter of an inch of wire. Now release the forceps and with a sharp pointed pair of scissors lift up a coil of your winding and snip off the surplus wire (*see* Fig 25). As you complete the process, the end of this coil will spring back into place, leaving a neat finish.

The second upper hook may be able to slide freely on the wire or it may be fixed. The sliding hook, as designed by Alfred Jardine, ensures that the trace is adjustable to suit various bait sizes. For our purposes, however,

A small pit 19½lb pike for Richard Reynolds.

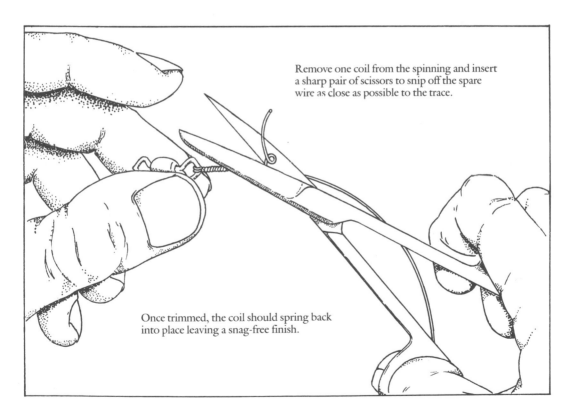

Remove one coil from the spinning and insert a sharp pair of scissors to snip off the spare wire as close as possible to the trace.

Once trimmed, the coil should spring back into place leaving a snag-free finish.

Fig 25   Trace making: trimming off stray end wire after spinning.

the fixed upper hook is preferred because it will not slip and damage the wire. Nor will it slip on the strike, which would reduce its effectiveness, particularly when fishing at extreme ranges.

To achieve this locked upper treble, follow the directions given in Fig 26. This shows exactly how to lay your wire to secure the hook at exactly the distance you require, to suit various bait sizes by half-inch increments from one and a half to three inches apart.

To finish the trace, fit the swivel just as you fitted the first hook attachment (*see* Fig 27). Feed the wire twice through the eye, leaving two inches of free wire, and then attach and spin the forceps to tightly spin the trace. Finally, cut off the remaining loose end by lift-ing the end coil (*see* Fig 25). This method of attaching hooks and swivels applies to all styles of trace, even spinning and lure traces. When all the spinning and trimming is com-plete, one final operation is required, and that is to test the trace.

Testing

Start the test by attaching a pair of forceps to the end treble or double hook. Take hold of these and grip the swivel, then stretch your arms apart and apply a firm pull on the whole trace. Do not be afraid to really pull – if the trace is going to break, it is better to do it now, rather than when you are attached to a big pike! This testing pull will settle the wire

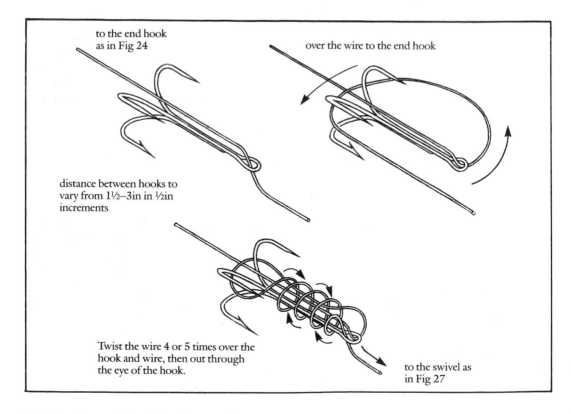

to the end hook
as in Fig 24

over the wire to the end hook

distance between hooks to
vary from 1½–3in in ½in
increments

Twist the wire 4 or 5 times over the
hook and wire, then out through
the eye of the hook.

to the swivel as
in Fig 27

Fig 26   Trace making: fixing the upper hook.

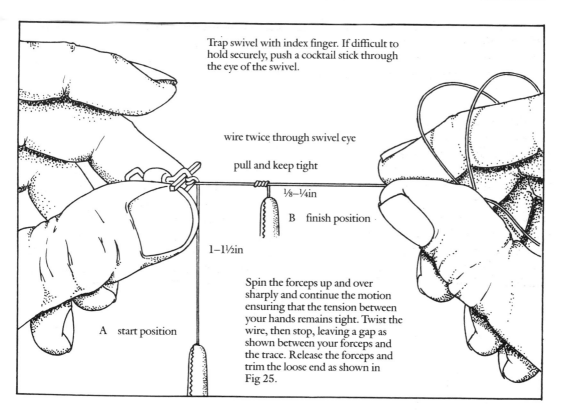

Trap swivel with index finger. If difficult to hold securely, push a cocktail stick through the eye of the swivel.

wire twice through swivel eye

pull and keep tight

⅛–¼in

B   finish position

1–1½in

A   start position

Spin the forceps up and over sharply and continue the motion ensuring that the tension between your hands remains tight. Twist the wire, then stop, leaving a gap as shown between your forceps and the trace. Release the forceps and trim the loose end as shown in Fig 25.

Fig 27   Trace making: swivel fixing.

round the second hook as well, which you will probably feel as a slight jerk. If nothing breaks, you have a trace ready for use. Now you should make up an assortment of various spacings, lengths, hook sizes and breaking strains ready to face any situation which might arise, testing each as it is made.

There are various ideas for the storage of these traces, but the most useful way is to wind them round a cylindrical or flat holder as shown in Fig 28. An occasional spray with WD40 will help protect them from rust as well, keeping them ready for use without tangles.

OTHER EQUIPMENT

Floats

Like most fishermen, pike anglers end up with a much larger collection of floats than they will ever need or use, but you will need a variety of floats to meet the demands of any situation that might confront you. Some of the more immediate requirements you will have are shown in the methods section in Figs 42 and 62. A full selection of the floats that you might find useful is illustrated in Fig 29. Some of these floats have only just become available and are designed for special purposes.

Sunset over the majestic Hickling Broad.

Landing Nets

Landing nets are always another point for discussion. Some advocate large, round frames whilst others say a large, triangular net is better. The main governing factors in the choice are availability and practicality. A triangular net with arms of thirty-six to forty-two inches will have the capacity to engulf the biggest pike you are likely to catch. The net should be of the tension cord, bow arm type that can be broken down easily for convenience and space, but still allow quick assembly when a fish is hooked. The length of the handle is another important factor – in fact, you may need two. If you fish from a lake or river bank you will need a handle of five to six feet in length, and if you also fish from a boat you will want a short twelve- to eighteen-inch handle. I recommend the new dual-mesh net. This has a large open mesh round the side, with a soft fine mesh for the bottom to save damage to your pike.

Keep Sacks

There was a time when having caught a large fish you might have felt the need to retain the fish until a camera was available, in which case you would probably have used a large keep net, but not today. In the interest of fish care you would be well advised to obtain a large keep sack, the same as a carp sack but larger, made of industrial nylon punched full of air holes, to retain your fish safely. This is much kinder than the mesh of a keep net. A new development in big pike retention is the pike tube. This is an advance on the keep sack and is a combination of the sack and the keep net, as illustrated in Fig 30. The advantage of this retainer is that both ends open and close with draw cords which allows easy entry and simple release. The tube is staked out in adequately deep water or tethered along the side of your boat. The pike is then visible at all times through the mass of punched holes which are all over the nylon covering.

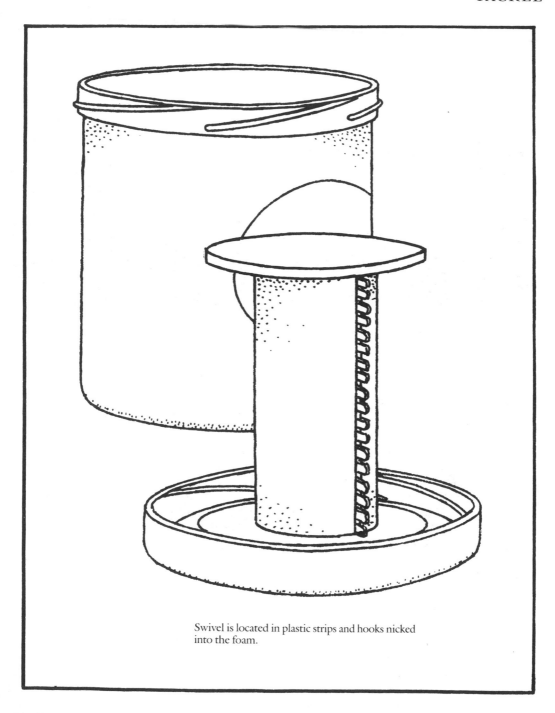

Swivel is located in plastic strips and hooks nicked
into the foam.

Fig 28   Trace tidy.

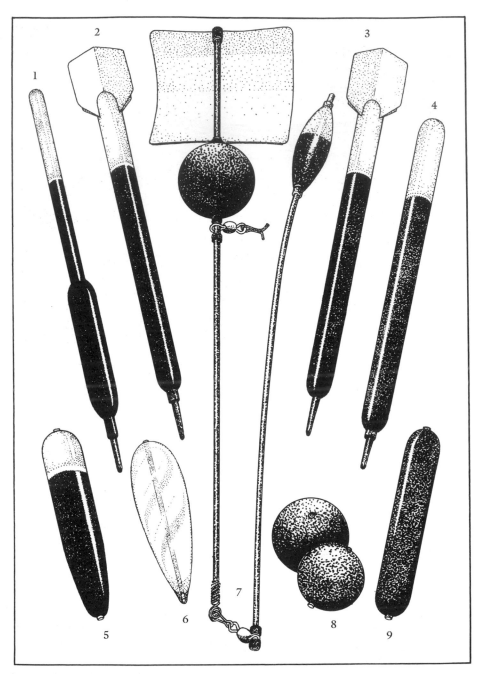

Fig 29 Assortment of floats. 1. Loaded windbeater float (Pike Tech). 2. Loaded vaned drifter float (Pike Tech). 3. Unloaded vaned drifter float (Pike Tech). 4. Loaded pencil float (Pike Tech). 5. Livebait super float (Pike Tech). 6. Clear subfloat (Drennan). 7. Super-controlled drift float (Pike Tech). 8. 1¼in and 1½in poly balls (Pike Tech). 9. Sunken pencil float (Pike Tech).

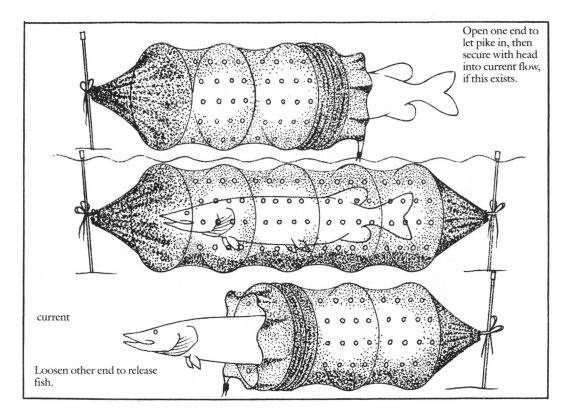

Open one end to let pike in, then secure with head into current flow, if this exists.

current

Loosen other end to release fish.

Fig 30   Pike tube (staked out).

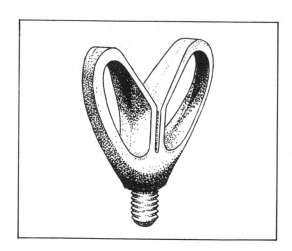

Fig 31   Rod rest head, seen from the front.

Extras

To make an effective start in pike fishing you will also require an assortment of adjustable rod rests with heads that allow free passage of line when a take occurs. An assortment of non-toxic arlesley weights from one to two ounces, some non-toxic zinc drilled bullets from half to one ounce, lengths of 1-mm ID silicon rubber, a supply of SSG (swanshot) in a non-toxic form, small-eye beads, a roll of 'power gum' for tying stop knots, a spool of five-pound line to tie paternoster links and a tub of Mucilin line floatant will also be very useful.

Fast, turbulent water of Tewkesbury Weir on the River Severn, an ideal winter venue.

View of a matured gravel pit.

Sunset view of the River Delph, one of Fenlands' most productive waters.

View of the approach to Lough Nafooey in Ireland.

4 Fisheries

BALANCING STOCKS

Good pike fisheries exist in spite of, rather than because of, good fishery management. So many of the waters that belong to angling clubs suffer from a culling policy where pike are openly persecuted because, as club officials like to put it, 'they only consume all the stock fish'. There is an easily-induced imbalance in any fishery created by club culls of big and medium-sized pike, which are caught more readily than the smaller fish. The following season there is then an upsurge in small pike, which become an even greater nuisance as they then decimate the smaller fish and fry, making the situation worse.

Good fishery management will view the overall population balance and note the value to the fishery of any predators that exist. Too many small pike will, as stated, cause a bigger problem than a few big pike. Whilst we need to preserve pike fishing, we must be prepared to accept that culling of many of the smaller fish of, say, less than four or five pounds will be beneficial to the growth of the bigger pike. This will, of course, be helpful to the pike angler, and will ultimately save the younger stock fish, such as roach and rudd, for the club angler who has no interest in pike as a species.

To be fair, some clubs and their committees are seeing the light and beginning to understand the benefits of balancing the stocks of their fisheries by retaining pike to cull off excessive quantities of small and sickly fish. The most vigilant in this matter, though, are the commercially-orientated fisheries who have recognised the value of the pike, not only in the balanced way of fishery management, but also in the fact that they can make revenue by allowing pike anglers to fish their waters during the otherwise inactive winter months, when takings are low.

More recent converts to this way of thinking are the commercially-run, 'put and take' trout fisheries. These are mainly the larger reservoir fisheries where there are also large coarse fish stocks. Many of these trout fisheries have regular nettings to reduce the coarse fish levels. These early nettings removed any size of pike, but the current trend is for a massive increase in small pike (many only two to three pounds in weight), to be netted. Although many thousands are removed each year, huge quantities of small pike remain.

The exception to this policy has been the experiment at Ardingley Reservoir in Sussex, where, despite the water being a prime trout fishery, the return of captured big pike is encouraged. There does not seem to have been any increase in the size of the pike population, nor any untoward effect on the trout fishing. The netting policies of the big reservoir trout fisheries have one benefit, in that they do, if organised properly, make good pike available for stocking into suitably sized general coarse fisheries. This has happened at gravel pits in Kent, Northampton and Cambridge, with fish caught or netted from Bewlbridge, Grafham and Rutland.

In your immediate area you will probably

Fig 32   Ardingley Reservoir – dam end.

find at least one, if not more, of the following types of fisheries: an established estate lake, gravel pit, reservoir or river. Within certain areas of the country, larger areas of water, such as lochs, loughs, broads and drains, have a value but all offer varying styles and qualities of pike fishing.

LOCATION

The best fishery to use will be the nearest one that offers good pike fishing and ideally, but not necessarily, contains a good head of larger fish. The nearer the fishery is to you, the more often and more easily you will be able to fish it and become familiar with it, in all of its moods throughout the season. Top-quality waters like Ardingley Reservoir in Sussex, or

maybe the Norfolk Broads, can produce fish over thirty pounds in weight, but they may be so far away from you that you cannot visit them frequently. Stick to your more local waters for regular sport, and pay the odd visit to these special waters if you wish, but remember the locals will have the advantage because they will have superior knowledge of the area.

TYPES OF FISHERY

You should find more than one fishery that has pike – the ideal would be three waters different both in location and characteristics. Taking three as a good number, you should locate, if possible, a shallow water fishery, a deep water fishery and maybe a river fishery.

The peace and quiet of winter on Broadlands' busiest stretch of river, the Bure at Wroxham.

Fig 33 Gravel pit fishery.

Fig 34 Tewkesbury Weir – river fishery.

This will give you access to some fishing throughout the winter months when weather conditions may make each fishery react in different ways.

Shallow Waters

The shallow estate-type lake or mere will warm up more quickly when mild spells occur in the winter, whereas the deeper waters will remain cool. This warming will activate the food fish shoals and in turn this will put the pike in a feeding mood. If you have acquired the correct knowledge about your fishery, you can go along to take advantage of the situation. These waters also fish well in the early winter and the last weeks of the season, when the pike shoal up for spawning. Another factor with these shallow waters is that they may be spring or brook fed. This water will usually be warmer than the main body of the lake, providing an ice-free area at the entry point, maintaining an area of fishable water.

This area may also be where the pike spawn, so it is worth checking at the right time.

The biggest disadvantage with the shallower water fisheries is that they often freeze over quite quickly, and in many cases stay frozen throughout the winter. This is where the other types of fishery come in useful. The deeper waters of a gravel pit or reservoir can, when combined with the wave action created by the wind across their open aspect, remain fishable in some very cold conditions. When the shallower areas fail to respond you can move on to the deeper areas which you should locate by plumbing. There is good sport to be enjoyed when you find your quarry feeding amongst the fry shoals that may have taken sanctuary in the warmer water – in some cases this can be twenty to thirty feet deep. If you are fortunate enough to locate what may prove to be a hot spot, you may well be able to maintain a consistent level of good pike fishing.

When the weather deteriorates to the point

Fig 35   Fenland drain – bridge in view.

where temperatures stay below zero for day after day, and all your stillwaters freeze and deny you your sport, it is then that you will be able to turn to your river fishery in the pursuit of yet more fish. Obviously, the river you choose will need to be of moderate size and flow to remain open during the coldest nights – slow deep rivers are likely to ice over just like your stillwater fisheries. Rivers with fast flows, weirs and those with tidal influences can prove very productive during even the coldest days, providing, of course, that the stretches you find actually contain pike! The thing to remember with river fisheries is that the pike in them are no different from still-water pike – you will find them where you find the roach and dace shoals.

Fenland Drains

Another system that can provide sport is the Fenland drains, such as the Sixteen-Foot Drain in Norfolk or the King's Sedgemoor in Somerset. The East Anglian drains do freeze like all waters, but sometimes the icing effects are reduced by pumping which creates conditions of flow, keeping the water open longer or re-opening it sooner.

Locate a good water, cultivate consistent sport by getting to know it and taking care of the fish. After all, you may be fishing a water that can produce what you are after, or even more.

5 Location and Feeding Habits

You can go to any water that contains pike, choose any swim and catch some fish, maybe even a big one if you have chanced to hit upon a hot spot. But you will probably not know *why* you have been lucky, and will probably find it very difficult to catch fish from other swims consistently when *the* swim is being fished by someone else. This is the trap so many average anglers fall into – they become single-swim, single-method anglers who occasionally catch a single fish!

To be more successful at locating and catching than the average pike angler, it is well worth spending your time researching your two or three chosen waters. Do not be tempted to fish every water in your area that contains pike, as you will only reduce the time you can spend on each and subsequently reduce the knowledge you gain of each. You need to get to know the water in every way possible: the depths, from the shallows to the deeper channels; the location of feeder streams or springs, if they exist; the location of bars, weed beds and sunken snags – in fact, just about anything that could be of some use in the location of feeding pike.

SEASONAL CHANGES

The time of year will certainly affect the location and feeding habits of the pike. In the course of a season there are some distinct changes in behaviour. From the beginning of the season, in June, and in each of the summer months of July, August and September, there is very little visible activity from the pike. This is mainly due to the fact that they are more evenly spread at this time of year and tend to use the cover afforded by generous weed growth to ambush their prey as they swim by. This is probably why summer catches are greater for the lure angler who exploits the opportunity of clear-water weed-bed fishing.

From the end of September, there is a tendency for pike activity to become more visible. From early October until December this hits a peak as the fish feel the onset of winter and feed ravenously in preparation for what may be several weeks of extremely low water temperatures. This activity usually coincides with weed beds dying and the fry shoals reaching their larger individual sizes. Without weed cover the fry become vulnerable to attack, the pike become preoccupied with this easy feeding and their activity becomes very visible with fry scattering on the surface. On days when pike are attacking near the surface, and swirls and boils are visible, it may be impossible to catch any pike unless you can present a similar sized bait amongst the fry shoals. Fig 40 shows a rig to offer a multiple bait in these conditions. All too frequently, no pike can be brought to the net, but it is worth persevering as you may locate some of the bigger fish by presenting a slightly larger bait at a depth a foot or two lower than the fry shoal.

As November arrives so do the first hard

Hot spot in the making? The construction of the Grafham Water aeration tower.

period sees a similar increase in pike anglers who, on witnessing such successes, will move in to capitalise on the spot you have revealed. Eventually this pressure drives the pike to move out in search of pastures new. Then, if you have learned anything from your research, you may know the most likely place to find them again and how to present a bait correctly in their new area.

As January arrives and passes into February, we often experience total freeze-ups. When this occurs a bait cannot be fished in many stillwaters. It is during the weeks when we approach the end of the season, as the thaw sets in, that the next phase of location begins. As the water temperatures rise to around 40°F (5°C), the pike begin to migrate from their deeper winter quarters to the shallow areas that will be slowly warming up in the spring sunlight, their intention being to congregate to spawn. The angler who knows his water can again capitalise by being ready to exploit what can be easier than average fish-

frosts, and the water temperatures fall, driving the fry and food fish into deeper water, followed closely by the pike. This is when all your research into contours and depths will pay dividends, because you will know where the fish may have gone, and will be able to identify which swims will offer the best opportunities of relocating them.

It is also possible that pressure from angling will drive the pike into new areas. Basically, when the fry shoals become confined to one area, so do the pike, and this can generate a seasonal hot spot which may produce some very large catches of good pike for the knowledgeable angler. Unfortunately, the same

Darren Cowles willing the indicators to drop and indicate a run.

Patience and good location pay off for young Darren Cowles.

ing, amongst tight shoals of pike preoccupied with the build-up of spawning. If you can locate the pike during this period, then you might expect to catch your heaviest fish of the season, and possibly your largest catch of fish, making all that effort pay real dividends.

RIVER FISHING

So far, we have only covered stillwater location, but much the same principles will apply to river pike location. However, there are some points worth noting if you intend fishing on rivers, particularly during the periods

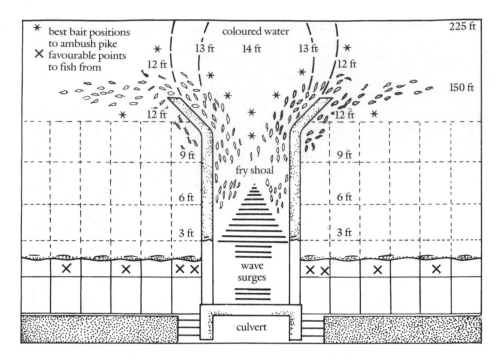

Fig 36   Reservoir fishery and swims.

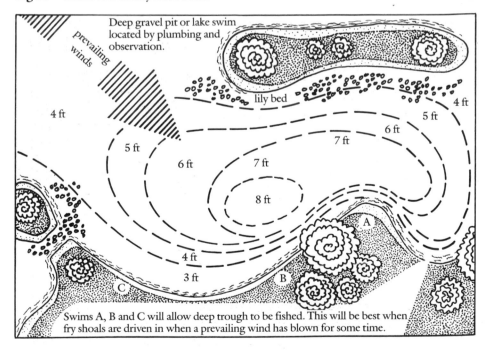

Fig 37   Gravel pit fishery and swims.

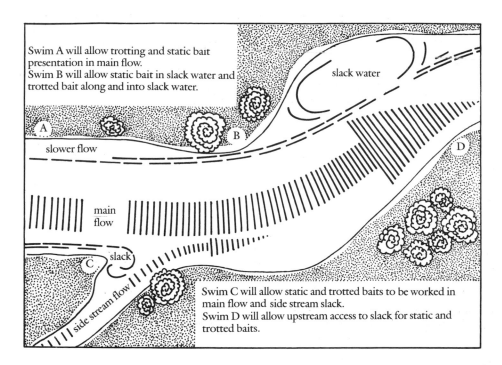

Swim A will allow trotting and static bait presentation in main flow.
Swim B will allow static bait in slack water and trotted bait along and into slack water.

slack water

A

slower flow

B

D

main flow

C slack

side stream flow

Swim C will allow static and trotted baits to be worked in main flow and side stream slack.
Swim D will allow upstream access to slack for static and trotted baits.

Fig 38   River fishery and swims.

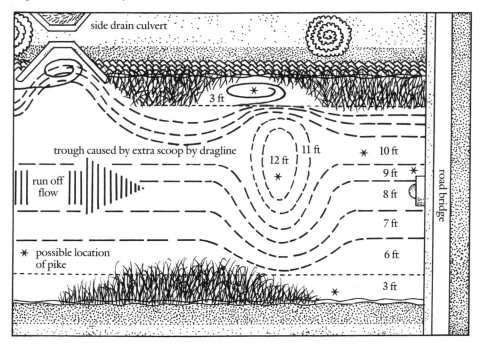

side drain culvert

3 ft

trough caused by extra scoop by dragline

11 ft

12 ft

10 ft

run off flow

9 ft

8 ft

7 ft

* possible location of pike

6 ft

3 ft

road bridge

Fig 39   Drain fishery and swims.

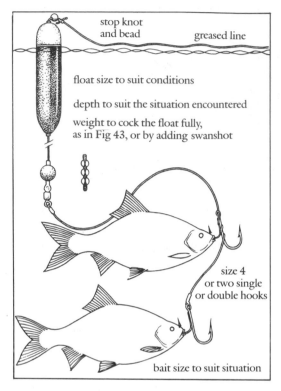

stop knot
and bead
greased line

float size to suit conditions

depth to suit the situation encountered

weight to cock the float fully,
as in Fig 43, or by adding swanshot

size 4
or two single
or double hooks

bait size to suit situation

Fig 40 Multiple bait rig, for livebait.

when the stillwaters are frozen. Generally, during the colder periods of winter it is unlikely that most rivers will be carrying flood or excess water – they are more likely to be low and clear with some lower reaches icing over in the hours of darkness. Even some of the upper reaches will freeze if they are not fast-moving. This tends to make fishing difficult, but when the temperatures do rise, the rivers quickly open up and fishing can be good again immediately after a short thaw commences – one which would not have had any effect on your stillwater. Ideally, you should be on the river both early and late to locate the roach and dace shoals, if they exist. The areas in which you find these, are those which you should concentrate on fishing.

During the winter months on tidal rivers, when there are periods of high tides the food fish will be pushed up into areas of river not too heavily affected by salt water. If you take the time to get to know your river, you can capitalise on these situations just as you would on your stillwaters. In times of flood on the rivers there are still chances to get amongst the pike, as the shoals of food fish will seek refuge from the strong current, and will be accompanied by numbers of pike (*see* Fig 38). Again, if you have taken time to research your favoured stretch of river, you will be able to predict some areas that will possibly hold a head of pike in a feeding mood. There could also be a deeper stretch of river bed, where a slack exists below the main force of flood water; or a slack area or back eddy on a bend where the main stream of current hits the opposite bank; or the mouth of a stream or drainage ditch which is flooded – try them all until you locate your quarry.

All this seems easy when you read it, but it is all too frequently forgotten. The only way to capitalise on this information in the future is to record *all* the data you acquire over the seasons in a log book. If you carefully note your successes and failures, and all other relevant data, you should be able to gain guidance from these in future seasons. Perhaps when you have tried other waters, which seemed promising enough to attract your attention, but failed to come up with the goods, you will find yourself returning to the old venues.

EFFECTS OF WEATHER CHANGES

Mild, damp and windy weather which can be associated with a low barometric pressure will have differing effects on waters, whether within a few miles of each other, or hundreds of miles apart. During these conditions, pike may be lethargic and unwilling to feed on a

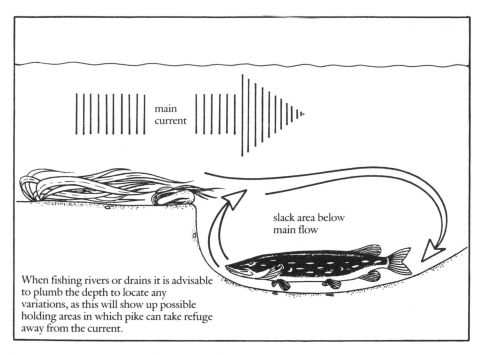

main current

slack area below main flow

When fishing rivers or drains it is advisable to plumb the depth to locate any variations, as this will show up possible holding areas in which pike can take refuge away from the current.

Fig 41   Deeper section of river bed or drain.

moving bait. In this case, they would be more likely to seek out a static deadbait. High barometric pressure which may bring cold frosty weather, clear skies and windless conditions, might see the pike more likely to seek out livebaits, although this will vary from water to water.

The one important factor you should remember is that the effects of prevailing weather conditions are only relative to your own local water or a water you may be seeking to fish. Fishing your waters in various conditions is the only real way to gain experience. As you can see, there is still more merit in understanding a water and having a range of known waters available to fish in the varying weather and seasonal conditions.

You can use knowledge of barometric pressure to your advantage by observing television and newspaper weather forecasts to identify the type of prevailing fronts, looking at the highs and lows on maps of the UK. By watching these daily, and studying your own barometer, you can establish whether there is a persistent high or low pressure front over your area, and identify the sort of response you will get from pike in your waters to livebaits, lures or deadbaits. A long-term low may give wind and rain and subsequently coloured water conditions. Deadbaits may then out-fish livebaits as the pike may be feeding by smell – remember the addition of flavourings and oils?

A long-term high pressure front may lead to clear water conditions, as frosts and low water temperatures will reduce algal colorations, making livebaits and lures a more viable proposition than deadbaits. But it is just possible that you could find that the reverse is true!

6 Deadbaiting

Deadbait fishing for pike undoubtedly first involved the use of dead coarse fish and eventually progressed to the use of dead sea-fish as they became more easily available through fishmongers, and more recently through specialist bait suppliers. The reported successes of well-known anglers taking big fish on sea deadbaits have had a big impact, but so have the Water Authority by-laws on live fish transferring and also the difficulty in obtaining supplies of bait fish from the waters being fished. The task of catching livebaits on even the warmer of winter days is daunting, so it is not surprising that many anglers have turned to using more sea deadbaits – and in turn, more captures of big pike to deadbaits are being reported. It all begins to look very easy: bait on the counter when you need it, most of it very freshly caught or at worst freshly frozen, thawed for sale. All you have to do is attach some hooks and cast out to catch yourself a pike.

Whilst publicity may have given you the answer to which bait is in vogue on which water, everyone else who reads the same article is now also using deadbaits on the same waters. This applies to all methods, livebaiting and lure fishing included. It all works well initially, then, as the fish get wise to baits, tackle and methods, the catches decline until no good fish are caught. What do you do? Do you change your bait? Do you try some new methods? Do you fish elsewhere? The answer is down to experience, and some basic knowledge of sound methods that you can use to overcome presentation problems. You must also use your own initiative to seek a new or different bait, be it flavoured, coloured, buoyant or even a different species, whilst others carry on with the blown baits and methods combination. The bait change is probably the easiest to effect, but sometimes it is purely presentation that causes the pike to reject your bait – this is where a good repertoire of methods will reap its greatest benefit.

HOOK SIZE AND POSITION

The hook size and its position on the bait are probably the greatest causes of failure in catching pike. In virgin waters or when ravenous, uninhibited feeding takes place, the presentation is of minor importance. But these circumstances are rare. It is more likely that you will find yourself fishing popular fisheries where the fish are very finicky. They will reject a bait with poorly positioned, over-sized hooks, but accept a correctly balanced hook and bait presentation in the same swim. Fig 7 illustrates some bait and hook layouts to suit a variety of bait sizes and types.

Basically, the hooks should balance to the size of bait, and this in turn should be balanced to the size of the pike you hope to catch under given circumstances. An eight-ounce herring on two size 6 trebles is not the ideal combination when you find the pike striking at shoals of fry in the surface layers of the water in question. A bait and hook combination as near to the size of the fish

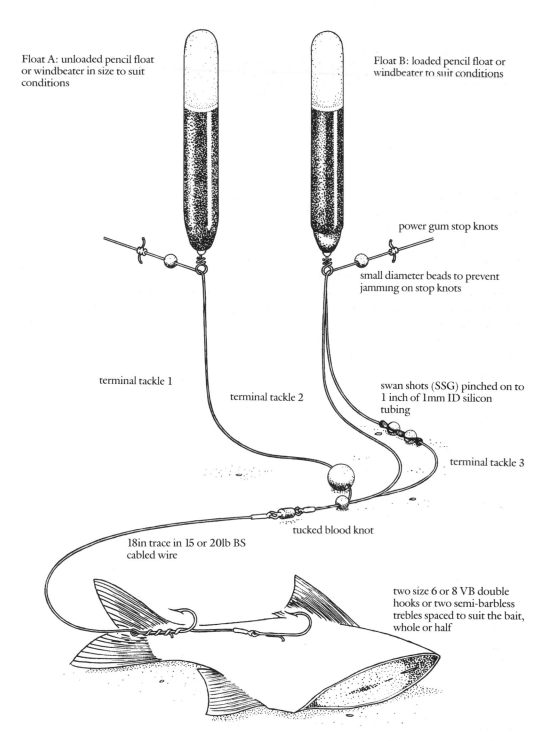

Float A: unloaded pencil float or windbeater in size to suit conditions

Float B: loaded pencil float or windbeater to suit conditions

power gum stop knots

small diameter beads to prevent jamming on stop knots

terminal tackle 1

terminal tackle 2

swan shots (SSG) pinched on to 1 inch of 1mm ID silicon tubing

terminal tackle 3

tucked blood knot

18in trace in 15 or 20lb BS cabled wire

two size 6 or 8 VB double hooks or two semi-barbless trebles spaced to suit the bait, whole or half

Fig 42   Float legering rigs.

57

Chris Turnbull and Dave Plummer take time off to coach some junior pike anglers at a
P.A.C. Teach-In.

making up the fry shoal as possible, or preferably just slightly larger, would be more suitable. This could then be presented as a buoyant
bait, legered on a longish trace in shallow
water or suspended under a float if in deep
water, set to a foot or two below the fry shoal.
The baits would be up to as much as three
ounces and could carry a single size 8 or size 6
semi-barbless treble in the tail, or two size 10
trebles, one in the dorsal and one in the pectoral.

The other examples in Fig 7 show balanced
bait and hook presentation for larger whole
baits and half baits, with sample hooking
styles. These, again, are examples and should
not be taken as hard and fast rules. If you wish
to use treble hooks instead of VB double
hooks, do so, but make sure that they balance
with the bait weight and length and are

strong enough to handle the largest size of
pike you may encounter in the water you are
fishing. You can be sure that Murphy's Law
will rule when you hook that thirty-pounder
on a size 10 fine wire hook in a snaggy swim.

Head sections of larger deadbaits are usually
left until there are no more tail sections left
and are then used reluctantly by many anglers,
but they will produce just as readily as tail
sections. It's a case of having the conviction to
use them! When mounting them, the upper
trace hook should go through both lips and
the other end should hook into the belly
section. The hooking arrangements shown in
Fig 7, will appear in the illustrations which
follow, and where necessary specific hooking
arrangements to suit the method will be discussed in more detail.

FLOAT LEGERING

The most popular method for deadbait fish is probably the float leger. Fig 42 shows two of the most widely used float arrangements and three terminal layouts. There are more permutations, but the methods discussed will serve you well – they are widely used by most experienced pike anglers. The most versatile in still and flowing water is a combination of Float B and terminal arrangement No. 3. The float is self-cocking and is six to eight inches in length. It is weighted to allow two to three inches to stand clear of the water, this portion being fluorescent-colour coated to make it highly visible. The swan shot is mounted on a thin silicon rubber tube placed on the line below the float, which stops the hard, non-toxic shot from damaging the line. The amount of rubber to use is approximately an inch in length. The amount of shot to use will be dictated by the distance to be cast or the bottom of the swim. If the bottom is silty you may choose to use no shot, as shown in terminal tackle No. 2, or just one SSG weight to counter the buoyancy of the bait.

In flowing water you can add SSG weights to enable the bait to just hold position in the water flow strengths you find on the day in question. The minimum amount you can use will make the presentation more sensitive and produce more pickups and subsequent runs than excessive weight. Terminal tackle No. 1 uses a drilled bullet, or perhaps a barrel lead – although with the banning of lead, these are now almost obsolete. Before mounting, the new zinc drilled bullet should be set on to a small-diameter plastic tube, as shown in Fig 43, and then locked on to the swivel with the silicon tube to give lifted bait registration, or left to slide on the line. The former method is preferred because it is best used with an unloaded, buoyant, bottom-only mounting float to register lift bites.

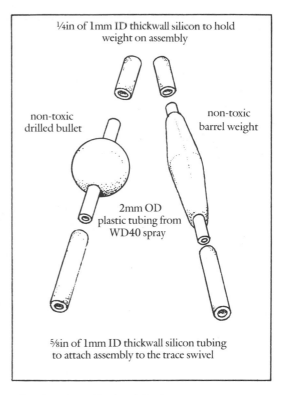

¼in of 1mm ID thickwall silicon to hold weight on assembly

non-toxic drilled bullet

non-toxic barrel weight

2mm OD plastic tubing from WD40 spray

⅝in of 1mm ID thickwall silicon tubing to attach assembly to the trace swivel

Fig 43   Trace fixed weight rig.

The bait illustrated in Fig 42 is a half bait, but it could easily be a full bait of any size. The hooks shown are VB double hooks and these have been set lightly into the skin of the bait to allow a quick firm strike to be made. If they were buried deep into the flesh of a bait such as fresh mackerel, with its tough skin, it could prove impossible to strike the hooks out, allowing a big pike to lever the hooks free of their hold by shaking the bait with its head. At long range, on a big bait, it is almost impossible to get a firm hook hold on the strike, so if you set the bait securely on the hooks for casting you must cater for this with your hook layouts.

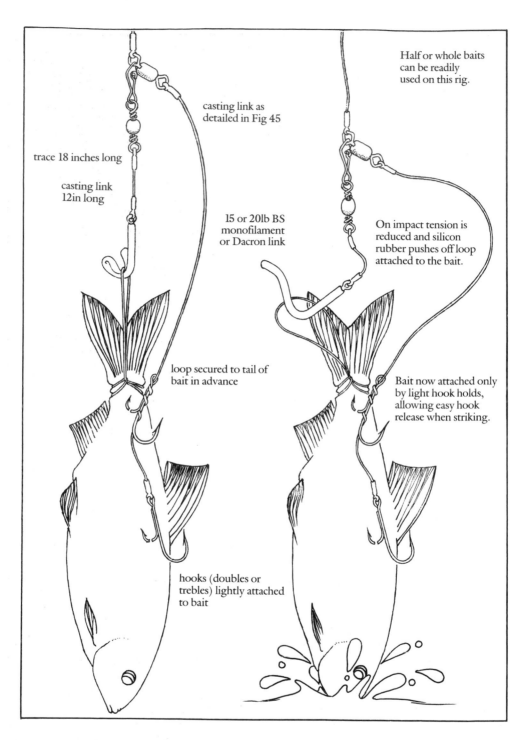

Half or whole baits can be readily used on this rig.

casting link as detailed in Fig 45

trace 18 inches long

casting link 12in long

15 or 20lb BS monofilament or Dacron link

On impact tension is reduced and silicon rubber pushes off loop attached to the bait.

loop secured to tail of bait in advance

Bait now attached only by light hook holds, allowing easy hook release when striking.

hooks (doubles or trebles) lightly attached to bait

Fig 44 Ejector rig layouts.

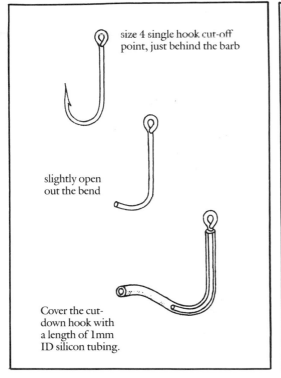

size 4 single hook cut-off point, just behind the barb

slightly open out the bend

Cover the cut-down hook with a length of 1mm ID silicon tubing.

Fig 45   How to make an ejector clip.

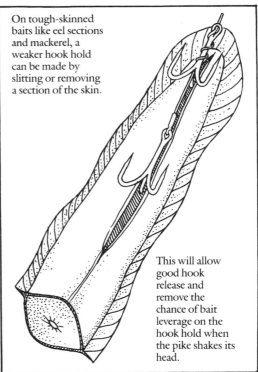

On tough-skinned baits like eel sections and mackerel, a weaker hook hold can be made by slitting or removing a section of the skin.

This will allow good hook release and remove the chance of bait leverage on the hook hold when the pike shakes its head.

Fig 46   Eel section with skin sliced.

BAIT EJECTOR RIGS

To keep the bait on the hook when casting, it is usually necessary to use large hooks firmly anchored in the tail root. The bait ejector rig, seen in Figs 44 and 45, allows light hook holds to be used, and whether you choose to use the VB double hook or equally balanced size trebles the principle is identical. Basically, the weight of the bait is taken by the loop secured around the tail of the bait, which can be made of any material that is at least as strong as the mainline. Dacron is ideal or, if necessary, you can use a loop of nylon line, although Dacron is less likely to slip and will not cut into the silicon rubber as easily as nylon.

This process of using the loop to take the weight is the secret of the ejector rig's simplicity. The compressed silicon loop or folded tube under load will ensure that the loop does not slip during the compression of the rod, throughout the cast and for most of the flight of your bait. As soon as the bait loses momentum and begins to fall, or when the bait hits the water, the silicon tube will automatically spring up and flick the loop off the hook. Providing you allow the bait to settle on the bottom, then slowly sink the line and cock your float, you will have a lightly hooked bait ready and waiting for that big fish – that is if you managed to cast into the desired spot. The only shortcoming in using light hook holds is that you may not get your bait if it should snag on the retrieve, but despite this, the method is worth using when the need arises. (The ejector rig is not restricted to use with this float rig but can be used with short- or medium-range straight legering.

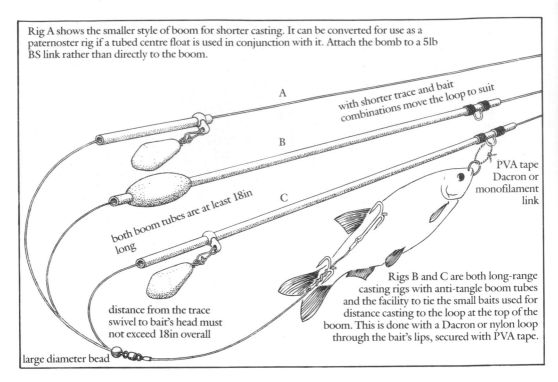

Rig A shows the smaller style of boom for shorter casting. It can be converted for use as a paternoster rig if a tubed centre float is used in conjunction with it. Attach the bomb to a 5lb BS link rather than directly to the boom.

A

with shorter trace and bait combinations move the loop to suit

B

both boom tubes are at least 18in long

C

PVA tape Dacron or monofilament link

distance from the trace swivel to bait's head must not exceed 18in overall

Rigs B and C are both long-range casting rigs with anti-tangle boom tubes and the facility to tie the small baits used for distance casting to the loop at the top of the boom. This is done with a Dacron or nylon loop through the bait's lips, secured with PVA tape.

large diameter bead

Fig 47 Long-range casting booms.

LONG-RANGE CASTING

Another question that is quite regularly asked is how can you cast a distance greater than fifty yards without tangling the bait and trace with the reel line during its flight. The answer is to use long-range legering, with casting rigs such as those shown in Fig 47. Rig A is a small casting boom, which either uses an all-plastic construction or alternatively a plastic tube through a large swivel, as shown on the paternoster rigs in Fig 62. Either variation is suitable for each method and will allow a quick change from float paternostering to leger fishing with a float by simply removing the paternoster link and fitting the bomb directly to the swivel on the boom – and vice versa from float leger to float paternoster. The use of this shorter boom is more in line with the intermediate ranges of fifty to sixty yards.

For greater range or for fishing into tight snaggy swims, use the boom Rigs B and C, as shown in Fig 47. These booms are a development from carp fishing where the tangling of baits as they trailed behind the bomb became a problem. Rig B shows a casting boom with an integral lead weight of approximately two ounces. Although the one shown is round in section, a boom with a fluted weight is also available, and is used where you need to hold the rig on the edge of a slope or gravel bar. It will also help in snaggy, weedy conditions as the fluting makes the rig rise quickly in the water.

Rig C is a similar rig, but here the bomb is attached to a link which means the weight can be varied – another important feature when fishing over weedy, silty lake beds.

On the long booms, the bait can be secured with PVA string. This is done by passing a

Gord Burton confidently holds and unhooks a Norfolk estate lake fish.

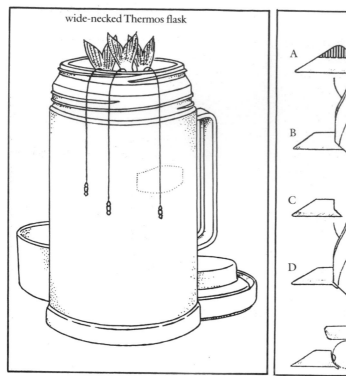

wide-necked Thermos flask

Fig 48 Thermos jar with trace mounted baits (frozen) for distance casting.

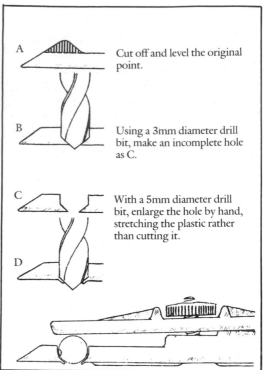

A   Cut off and level the original point.

B   Using a 3mm diameter drill bit, make an incomplete hole as C.

C   With a 5mm diameter drill bit, enlarge the hole by hand, stretching the plastic rather than cutting it.

D

Fig 49 Modified line clip.

length of Dacron or similar material through both lips of the bait to form a loop, and then securing this with PVA string to the adjustable loop on the boom. The boom will probably be eighteen to twenty-four inches in length, so with a fifteen to eighteen-inch trace you can tension the trace and bait up tight by sliding the loop up along the boom, taking up all the unnecessary slack. When the rig hits the water the PVA will dissolve and in a few minutes the bait will be loose. If it is a buoyant bait it will then rise into position; if it is a heavy-bottom bait a slight retrieve of two to five feet of line will take the boom clear of the bait and trace and leave the bait ready for a pike to pick up.

BITE INDICATORS

The bait is now in position and ready for action. The best method of bite indication in these conditions is the drop back, arm-type indicator. Either use just a visual indicator, or an audible indication as well, attached to the back rod rest. There is a very definite need for both lift and drop back indication with this and all pike fishing methods. Where a float is not possible then the indication must be positive. This is best achieved close to the reel so that very little resistance is felt after the initial movement of the indicator is made, particularly if the pike moves off with the bait. We must obtain maximum confidence from the pike if it is not to reject the bait.

Monkey-climber-type indicators in damp conditions bind on the needle and create resistance. The possibility of this happening with the adjustable clip drop arm indicator illustrated is minimal. Once the line is pulled from the modified, lightly adjusted clip (Fig 49), line can be freely pulled off the spool because the bail arm is left open. All that is needed then is for the bail arm to be closed, and as there is nothing else on the line, it is a simple matter of tightening up and pulling home the hooks.

The arrival of these two indicators has really made all the others obsolete. If you own an optonic-type indicator, this can be employed with the visual indicator shown. Although you will have the disadvantage of a variety of false indications from the wind and undertow tension on the line, even this is more acceptable than deep-hooked fish. Pike have a habit of giving drop back indication as frequently as they give lift-type bite indic-ation, so a weighted arm indicator can pull back the slack line and indicate the instant the bait moves when it is picked up.

FREE-ROVING FLOAT RIGS

The mobile approach of using a suspended bait, fished under a float, is often not used to its full potential. Many just attach a set of trebles to the bait, usually under the old and totally outdated Gazette Bung, then cast out and leave the rest to chance. The method of fishing a deadbait under an untethered float or, as it is known when using livebait, a free-roving float rig, is one that should be used more, as it is more likely, if used correctly, to locate more pike in the course of a day than a static deadbait. With the development of legering techniques this method seems to have been neglected, perhaps because it takes more effort to do correctly, or maybe because it requires more attention and skill to get the best from it than legering does.

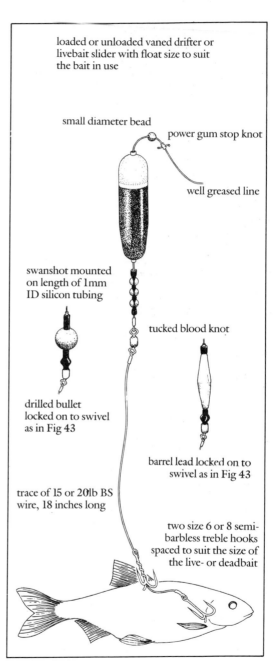

loaded or unloaded vaned drifter or livebait slider with float size to suit the bait in use

small diameter bead

power gum stop knot

well greased line

swanshot mounted on length of 1mm ID silicon tubing

tucked blood knot

drilled bullet locked on to swivel as in Fig 43

barrel lead locked on to swivel as in Fig 43

trace of 15 or 20lb BS wire, 18 inches long

two size 6 or 8 semi-barbless treble hooks spaced to suit the size of the live- or deadbait

Fig 50 Untethered, free-roving rig, for live and deadbait.

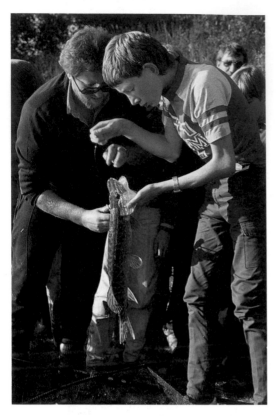

Dave Plummer shows young Paul Gribble the confident way to unhook his pike, taken during a P.A.C. Teach-In.

The general untethered, free-roving bait rig shown in Fig 50 is for use with deadbaits and livebaits on still and moving waters in lakes and rivers. Gone is the bulbous body of the old bung, to be replaced by the slim-bodied float illustrated, which is again finely balanced with either SSG weights, fixed drilled bullets or barrel leads to make the float just support the bait, as used in static deadbaiting. Resistance will cause a pike to reject a bait – the same is true with float buoyancy, as too much will create resistance when the pike retreats back down to the lake or river bed to deal with the bait it has seized. You will often notice after the bait is taken that the float disappears only to pop back up again, and in many cases stays there. When you eventually decide to strike, usually after several minutes of trying to decide if in fact you have a bite, you wind in and find a tooth-marked bait. In most cases that bait was probably rejected due to float resistance or unbalanced hook to bait sizes, or both. Finely balanced tackle and bait will give you a greater chance of success, than unbalanced, carelessly presented tackle.

Bait Mounting

The deadbait is mounted in the same way as you might mount livebaits, with one hook (the upper treble) in behind the dorsal fin, and the other in the flank in front of the pectoral fin, to give the deadbait a similar attitude to a live fish in the water. To achieve this with sea-fish baits requires no special action, but when using dead coarse fish you will have to puncture the swim bladder and then squeeze the air from the body, otherwise the bait will be suspended above the weights. If the pike then seizes the bait, it could also catch the reel line, which would most likely break or be cut on its teeth, leaving the fish to swallow not only the bait but the hooks as well. Hooks trapped in the pike's throat may cause its death by preventing it from feeding. So remember to pierce the swim bladder on all coarse fish if you intend float fishing in this manner.

Drifting

This style of fishing allows you to cover large areas of water if there is a wind blowing, whether you are on the bank of a river, lake or in a boat, providing that the line above the stop knot, which sets the depth, is greased with Mucilin line floatant. Not only does this floating line cause the line to drift with the wind and tow the float and bait around, but it will

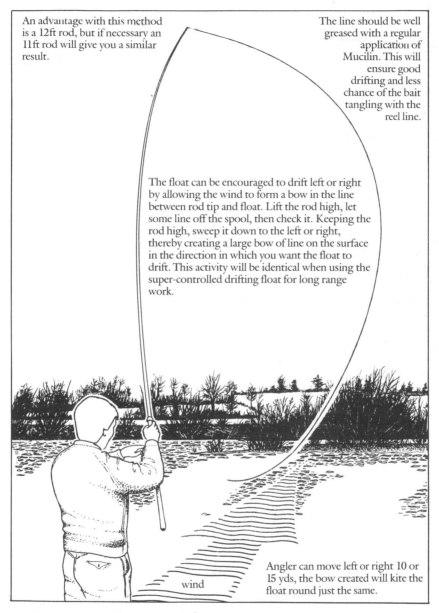

An advantage with this method is a 12ft rod, but if necessary an 11ft rod will give you a similar result.

The line should be well greased with a regular application of Mucilin. This will ensure good drifting and less chance of the bait tangling with the reel line.

The float can be encouraged to drift left or right by allowing the wind to form a bow in the line between rod tip and float. Lift the rod high, let some line off the spool, then check it. Keeping the rod high, sweep it down to the left or right, thereby creating a large bow of line on the surface in the direction in which you want the float to drift. This activity will be identical when using the super-controlled drifting float for long range work.

wind

Angler can move left or right 10 or 15 yds, the bow created will kite the float round just the same.

Fig 51 Control of float using wind.

also prevent the line tangling with the bait and hooks by sinking, as most monofilament line does.

The float can be encouraged to drift by laying a bow in the line by lifting the rod high after the cast, as shown in Fig 51, and allow-ing the wind to pull the line in the same direction. Then lower the rod quickly in the direction in which you wish the float to go, and eventually the float will swing slowly round till the line tightens. If you wish, you can then repeat the whole procedure and lift

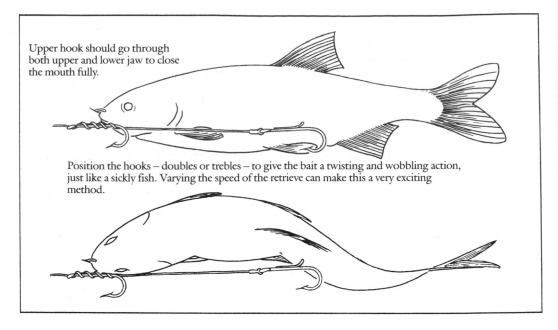

Upper hook should go through both upper and lower jaw to close the mouth fully.

Position the hooks – doubles or trebles – to give the bait a twisting and wobbling action, just like a sickly fish. Varying the speed of the retrieve can make this a very exciting method.

Fig 52   Wobbled bait mounting.

another loop into the wind extending your float's drift. At the end of this chapter a further drifting technique will be dealt with which will enable you to drift greater distances. The technique of getting your deadbait and float to move is identical if you are working from a boat.

Depth of Float

If you know nothing about the chosen swim you should start by fishing your bait at a depth of approximately three feet. After each unsuccessful swing round you should try the next cast with the bait lowered by twelve inches, and then progressively lower your bait until it either produces a take or snags on the bottom. Once you have reached the bottom you can then reduce the depth by a foot and continue searching the area thoroughly, by perhaps moving ten yards to the left or right, if it is possible, and then vary the depth again to try and locate your quarry.

WOBBLE AND SINK AND DRAW DEADBAITS

The most active of deadbait methods are wobble, and sink and draw deadbaits. There is nothing more exciting than getting a take on the retrieve of a moving bait – the rod is almost wrenched from your hands as the pike strikes, maybe under the rod top. The most important point with this method is the way the bait is mounted, and Fig 52 details how to locate the hooks, through both lips, with either trebles, or as shown with size 8 or 6 VB double hooks. The end treble serves a very important dual purpose. Firstly, it actually holds the bait in a curved shape, which imparts a waggling action into the bait; secondly, being positioned well back and low on the bait, it will usually be the hook that finds a good hold in the pike's lower jaw where the softer flesh is. The method is ideal to use when pike are seen chasing fry shoals within casting distance, for raising fish that do not respond to other less active methods

Vary the rate of retrieve and style of action to create an enticing action in your bait. Pull hard, stop to let the bait flutter down, then pull again and so on until it is fully retrieved.

Buoyant bait and non-buoyant baits can be used to give different actions. Both should be tried to gain the best results.

Try this method in close to reed beds, lily beds, weed beds or snaggy areas that might hold a waiting pike. Work the bait over the same area 3 or 4 times at least.

Fig 53 Action of wobbled or sink and draw bait.

and for work along the margins by lily beds, reed beds and snags where pike may be taking cover.

You can also put some action into the bait after casting by sharply tugging the bait at different speeds and places. Then, between each action, allow the bait to sink slowly, so that its fluttering action will soon entice and raise pike if they are in the area. You should cast the bait to the same spot at least three or four times, because each successive cast will, if it is covering a pike, entice a take. You might notice a slight jerk on maybe the third retrieve, in which case you should then try the same spot once or twice more – you will probably find that the next take is the one that hooks your pike.

If, after four casts, nothing happens, cast to a new position. From your standpoint, imagine the area in front of you is half a clock face showing from nine through to three, and cast to each of the hour positions. Then move fifteen to twenty yards along the bank and repeat the process. Working from a boat you can move round the boat by the same hour point positions covering a large area, then move your boat thirty yards or so back, forward or sideways until you cover some pike. Wobble, and sink and draw fishing of deadbaits is well worth the time, particularly when things are slow – you may even locate a hot spot or holding area in which you can place your deadbaits or livebaits.

Free-roving livebait rig, set shallow to work over weed beds on the Norfolk Broads.

A drift-caught 27½lb trout-water pike for Kevin Grix.

7 Livebaiting

On most waters the use of livebait is restricted to fish caught from the water being fished. Even so, the controlling club or authority may or may not allow the use of livebaits, so before considering the use of livebait, take into account the prevailing circumstances and choose waters where there are no immediate restrictions. Make every effort *not* to draw attention to the use of livebait by using either excessively large quantities or sizes of bait. The transfer of fish from water to water is universally prohibited and covered by specific by-laws. However, with care and consideration for this fact, there is no reason why you should experience any difficulty.

The recommended size for livebaits outlined by many pike anglers is up to four ounces, and this is a very reasonable and realistic size for use. At the extreme, if you should happen to be catching five-ounce fish you might consider using a few, but do not use any excessively large ones. The chances are that these may be the source of your smaller fish – remove the breeding stock and you remove your future bait supply. Do not be afraid to lower your size limit either, because whilst three- to four-ounce livebaits look very attractive to us as anglers, in many cases the pike will probably be preoccupied with feeding on shoals of fry, or second- and third-year-class fish which may weigh only one or two ounces, and may subsequently ignore your large bait.

CATCHING BAIT

To catch your bait you should locate a pond, lake or stretch of river that is very well stocked, or overstocked with fish, so that the quantity of bait you will take during the course of the season will not cause the water to suffer. In some areas fry recruitment, particularly on some of our non-tidal rivers, is very limited, if not totally non-existent, notably in the cases of roach and dace. Remember you may not be the only angler fishing for livebait on your chosen water, so take only what you need to give an adequate supply, and remember that overcrowding your bait bucket and bait tank will rob you of your hard-earned bait due to lack of oxygen, hastening your return to catch more. If the venue is out of condition or frozen you will not get very many, if any, so take only those you really need.

The number you should take will be decided by how much you intend fishing. There is absolutely no point holding a hundred in a tank if you will only fish a few weekends during the winter seasons. However, that could in fact be a reasonable quantity for an average winter from November to mid-March – remember that some waters will be frozen and you may not get to fish anyway, so any more bait would be excessive. A suggested initial quantity would be twenty, adding ten or so more on each trip out if you catch them. But do not be greedy and take too many, and do not overstock your tank.

Fig 54   Bait-carrying containers.

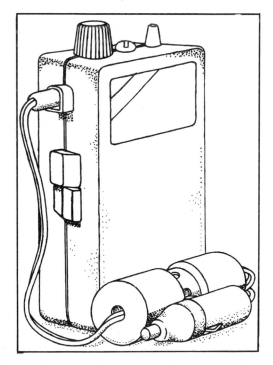

Fig 55   Dual voltage aerator and battery adaptor.

STORAGE AND TRANSPORT

Those fish which you retain should be kept in such a way that they remain in good condition. Obviously a fresh, lively bait will work harder for longer than a battered, sickly bait. Also, baits unused at the end of the session, if you have caught them on the water being fished, or else at the end of the season, can be returned to the water in good condition with an excellent chance of survival. There is nothing worse than witnessing a lot of dead rudd and roach that have been tipped back by pike anglers who have kept bait badly. Respect your bait fish as much as you respect your quarry. Pike angling needs to present its image in the best possible way, and conservation of bait fish is as important as conservation of pike stocks. Some anglers get as much of a thrill out of catching a four-ounce roach as you will from catching a ten-pound pike.

To help the conservation of bait it is advisable to equip yourself with a three- to

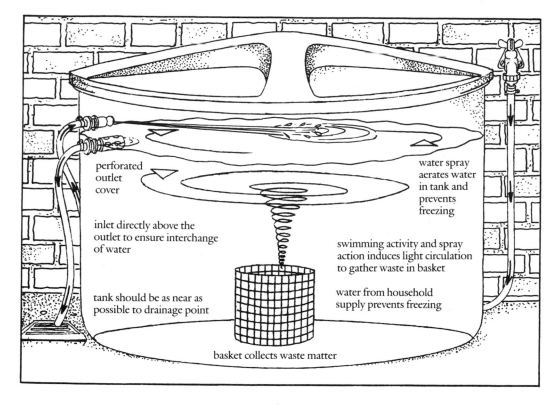

perforated
outlet
cover

inlet directly above the
outlet to ensure interchange
of water

tank should be as near as
possible to drainage point

water spray
aerates water
in tank and
prevents
freezing

swimming activity and spray
action induces light circulation
to gather waste in basket

water from household
supply prevents freezing

basket collects waste matter

Fig 56   Bulk storage tank layout.

five-gallon bait bucket and a good quality, dual-voltage aerator, in which you can retain and carry your bait. An important tip which will help the survival of the bait you catch is not to handle the fish at all with dry hands. If you are catching them with rod and line, have your bait bucket filled in front of you and as you catch your bait, swing it into the bucket and unhook it in the water. If you remove even a small amount of the natural slime from the body of your bait, you will allow a fungus to grow which may kill the fish, so do *not* dry handle your bait.

From the bucket your bait will be readily accessible, and can be netted out when required. If you retain your bait in a keep net, every time you pull up your net to get a bait you will disturb all the others, causing scale displacement and stress. When you throw the

keep net back out, the bait will suffer further stress and impact damage, resulting in loss or injury which will inhibit the attractive action of a tethered bait. This will ensure that the seagulls and rats get a good supper, and pike angling receives a bad name. So, protecting your bait will ultimately protect your pike fishing.

Home Storage

To store baits at home you will need to organise a sound, healthy approach to bait tanks. The functional type of holding tank shown in Fig 56 will ensure a regular change of water, and the spray action keeps the water aerated. This is also a great aid in preventing the water from freezing in the depth of winter, because it is continually moving, and if it is taken from the household supply it will be at quite a few degrees above freezing point. This water also keeps the outlet from freezing up. The basket in the centre supplies a filtering action to gather the matter excreted by newly-stocked baits – the continual circular swimming of your bait will generate a slack area in the centre of the basket in which the rubbish will accumulate. Cleaning this out once a week or so with a siphon tube or a small bilge pump run from a car battery is simple, ensuring again that no noxious, toxic waste (ammonia) can build up and kill your bait. The tank should be no more than three-quarters full, the level being set by the outlet, which should be screened against blockage by means of a piece of mesh clipped over the fitting or the edge of the tank. The inlet point should be directly over the outlet to ensure that the water circulates before it leaves by the outlet. The tank should be sited as near to a drain and water supply as possible, and be screened against any freezing winter winds by four surrounds, or better still placed in a garage or shed.

FREE-ROVING RIGS

Probably the most popularly used method in livebait fishing is the free-roving method as illustrated in Fig 50 for use with deadbaits. The tackle needed is very similar to the untethered rig for deadbaiting described previously, with the exception that with a livebait, the rig can be made to move upwind by using the bow in the line caused by the wind to generate some resistance. This will pull against the bait, and encourage it to swim in the opposite direction, which in many cases will be against the wind.

The hook position when using livebaits is again important in bait rejection. The best answer is to adopt a balanced approach to bait, hook size and layout of traces, and also the positioning of hooks in the bait (*see* Figs 57 and 58). Hook positioning is important, as when seizing a live, wriggling bait, the pike will be unlikely to reject it unless the bait hook size is out of balance. With a four-ounce bait you can safely use up to two size 6 semi-barbless trebles, correctly positioned. The optimum hook size will be a pair of size 8 semi-barbless trebles, which for slow moving rivers and stillwaters should be positioned midway along the bait, with the upper treble at the front of the dorsal and the end hook tucked in the flank just in front and above the pectoral fin. To allow the bait to swim more naturally in fast moving waters, the upper treble should go through the top lip and the end treble in the flank, just in front of and below the pelvic fins. Smaller baits will require smaller hooks – do not try mounting large baits on small hooks as this will result in lost baits on the cast.

Layout

The layout of the free-roving livebait rig makes it ideal for livebait trolling in slower moving rivers as well, and to some degree in stillwaters that have adequate depth. Fig 59 shows how the rig is fished, basically by extending the length to fish just slightly over depth. The bait is suspended off the bottom by the speed of the trolling boat.

The free-roving bait can be used just about anywhere in either of its styles, the only restriction being that it should not be fished where the bait could possibly become snagged. Anywhere that a bait or a pike can swim is suitable for the use of the free rover. It will, with a well-greased line, work its way around the area of your swim at any depth you select.

When working in flowing water where there is a strong wind against the flow, there is

Mike Woods with an estate lake 19½lb fish.

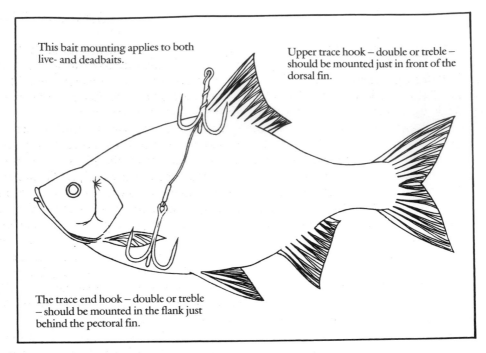

This bait mounting applies to both live- and deadbaits.

Upper trace hook – double or treble – should be mounted just in front of the dorsal fin.

The trace end hook – double or treble – should be mounted in the flank just behind the pectoral fin.

Fig 57   Stillwater livebait hook position.

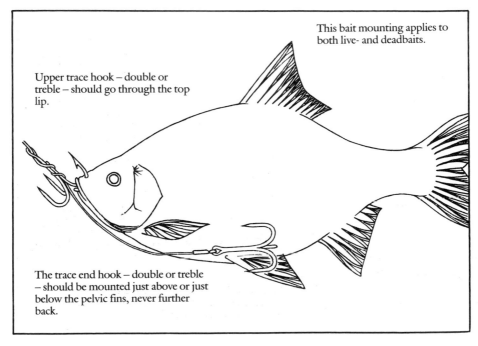

This bait mounting applies to both live- and deadbaits.

Upper trace hook – double or treble – should go through the top lip.

The trace end hook – double or treble – should be mounted just above or just below the pelvic fins, never further back.

Fig 58   River rig livebait hook position.

a possibility that your float may be held back by drag on the line. To solve the problem you will need a fluted cigar-shaped float, as shown in Fig 60, if you can locate one. The idea behind the design is that the water cannot slip round the float body, as it does on a round section float, and it will therefore be driven by the flow, against the wind. The wind does not have the same effect on the other side as it is not solid – the pressure from the water is a stronger force. The float illustrated is a useful item of tackle if you are ever confronted with the problem when fishing on a river.

FLOAT PATERNOSTERS

Where the problem of snags exists in close proximity to pike, the method to use instead of the free-roving rig is the float paternoster rig. This method is illustrated fully in Fig 62, which shows the various float options. Many more styles of float paternoster rigs exist, but the method illustrated has recently become the most successful of them all.

The paternoster can be used either with surface or sunken floats. Three float types are shown – the one on the left is a bottom-only mounted float which will allow the line to be fished sunken to prevent the effect of drag pulling the float down or out of position. The centre float is a polyball of about one and a half inches in diameter and, as shown, it is specifically for sunken float use. The float on the right is a tubed centre sliding float which can be fished with a greased line in shallow water down to a depth of four feet – the floating line will prevent the bait tangling with a sunken line. All these can be used as sunken floats by simply setting them under depth.

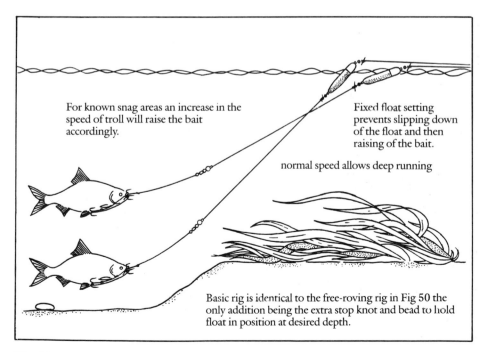

For known snag areas an increase in the speed of troll will raise the bait accordingly.

Fixed float setting prevents slipping down of the float and then raising of the bait.

normal speed allows deep running

Basic rig is identical to the free-roving rig in Fig 50 the only addition being the extra stop knot and bead to hold float in position at desired depth.

Fig 59   Trolling variation of free-roving rig and its use.

Trotting a bait through a deep bend of a Suffolk river.

Sunken Floats

The most important thing to remember with sunken floats is to have just enough weight to sink the float. Most polyball floats seem to work well with around 1½-ounce bombs on the paternoster link. Remember to use beads between all swivels and tubes to prevent the jamming of tackle on stop knots. The surface float allows visual indication of activity during your wait for a take, and it will also indicate the take itself.

This method will be limited by the depth of the water you are proposing to fish. If the water is over eight feet deep, the sunken float

paternoster method is more practical, indeed some pike anglers use this method exclusively in any depth of water. The main advantage is that there is no need to plumb your water to find the depth – you simply set your float to fish at approximately eight to ten feet, including a three-foot paternoster link, and cast into your chosen swim. If the water is shallower choose a setting six to twelve inches below the surface. Paternostering is not advisable in water shallower than three feet, and up to depths of six feet a fixed float should be used to prevent tangling of the bait with your reel line, with the risk of a bite-off when a pike strikes. You can use the sunken paternoster as an indicator to locate any shallow areas or gravel bars when retrieving slowly. If you let the float cock properly you can then position

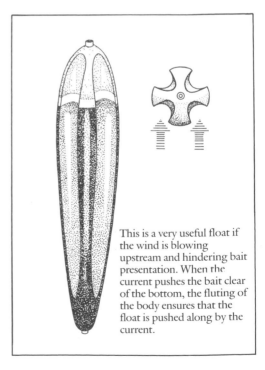

This is a very useful float if the wind is blowing upstream and hindering bait presentation. When the current pushes the bait clear of the bottom, the fluting of the body ensures that the float is pushed along by the current.

Fig 60   Fluted trotting float.

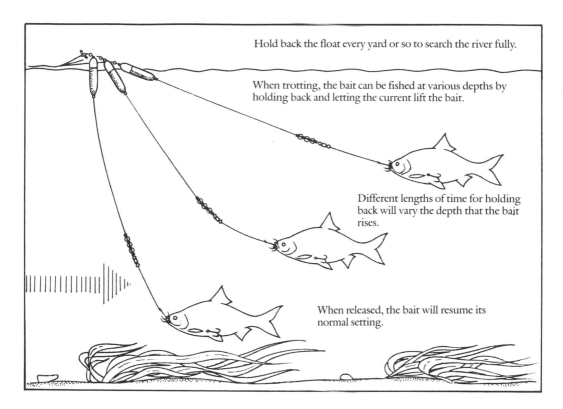

Hold back the float every yard or so to search the river fully.

When trotting, the bait can be fished at various depths by holding back and letting the current lift the bait.

Different lengths of time for holding back will vary the depth that the bait rises.

When released, the bait will resume its normal setting.

Fig 61   Trotting a livebait in a river.

your baited rig in the supporting gullies when one of these has been noted.

Despite not being a mobile, searching method like a free-roving livebait, the float paternoster is usually the method used to present a bait in a likely swim and hold it there (*see* Figs 63 and 64 for examples of likely swims). A free-roving bait is likely to move away from a pike-holding spot or patrol feature like shelves or gravel bars whereas a paternostered bait will be placed into the spot you wish. It will then be held exactly where you put it and only move to the extremes that the trace length will allow. If you're fishing a surface paternoster, that movement may be greater if you have not got your depth correct – if you're over depth by one or two feet you

may just allow your bait to get into snags you are fishing against or delay bite indication and allow the pike to be deep hooked – so make sure you have the rig set to the correct depth.

However, with sunken float paternosters you are assured of two very important advantages: firstly, you will always have a tight line between trace and float; secondly, with the use of drop back, lift arm bite indicators, you will be able to spot the exact moment your bait is seized by the pike, and proceed to set the hooks before the bait is swallowed. When using either method you should always ensure that you use a stop knot between the float and trace at a distance at least twelve inches greater than the trace length. This will prevent the bait tangling with the float during

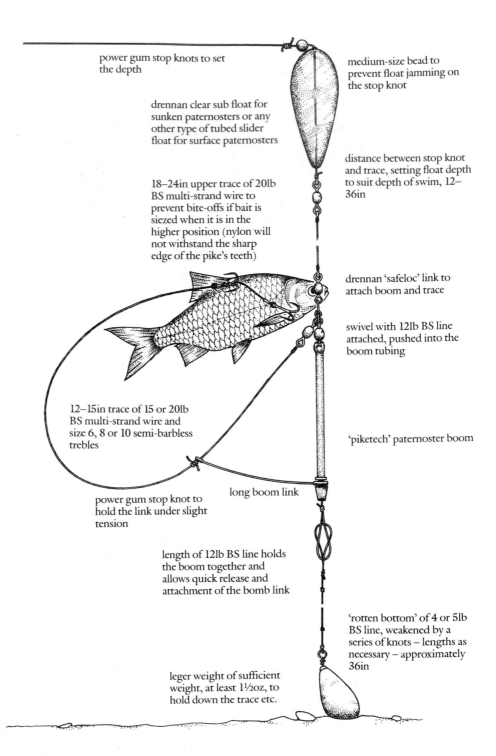

power gum stop knots to set
the depth

medium-size bead to
prevent float jamming on
the stop knot

drennan clear sub float for
sunken paternosters or any
other type of tubed slider
float for surface paternosters

18–24in upper trace of 20lb
BS multi-strand wire to
prevent bite-offs if bait is
siezed when it is in the
higher position (nylon will
not withstand the sharp
edge of the pike's teeth)

distance between stop knot
and trace, setting float depth
to suit depth of swim, 12–
36in

drennan 'safeloc' link to
attach boom and trace

swivel with 12lb BS line
attached, pushed into the
boom tubing

12–15in trace of 15 or 20lb
BS multi-strand wire and
size 6, 8 or 10 semi-barbless
trebles

'piketech' paternoster boom

long boom link

power gum stop knot to
hold the link under slight
tension

length of 12lb BS line holds
the boom together and
allows quick release and
attachment of the bomb link

'rotten bottom' of 4 or 5lb
BS line, weakened by a
series of knots – lengths as
necessary – approximately
36in

leger weight of sufficient
weight, at least 1½oz, to
hold down the trace etc.

Fig 62   Paternoster rig layouts.

Fig 63   Paternoster swim (gravel bar).

casting and rule out the chance of a bite-off occurring.

Bite Indicators

When using either style of paternoster, but particularly with the sunken float, you will require an alternative means of bite registration, preferably an audible/visual type or at least a visual type as illustrated in Fig 65. Those pictured are both of the stiff-arm type with adjustable line clips and large-sized sight bobbins. They should both be set on the back rod rest directly below the reel spool, and be set low enough to indicate tight line bites as well as full pull-out bites and the so common drop-back type bite.

When fishing sunken floats you should take great care to set both these indicators properly. After casting to your chosen spot, wind down tight to sink your line, then release the bail arm and allow the line off the spool until it goes slack. This will ensure that the float rises fully vertically. Now place the rod in the rod rest with it pointing directly at your bait, close the bail arm and slowly recover the slack line until it just lifts off the water. Attach your drop arm indicator and tighten the clip. If there is any slack the indicator will fall back, so rotate the spool to wind the line and indicator up until it sits level as in Fig 66. Then pull it down fully and if you have a tight line between the rod and float it will rise slightly under tension. If it does not, wind up some more line on to the spool and repeat until the indicator resets after you release it. With the indicator set up this way you will register instantly any activity by a pike striking at your bait, either by the arm rising sharply, dropping back slowly or dropping back free if the pike grabs and runs off with your bait. With the audible/visual indicator illustrated, the 'Predator', the arm mechanism is designed to be very sensitive so that it will indicate very

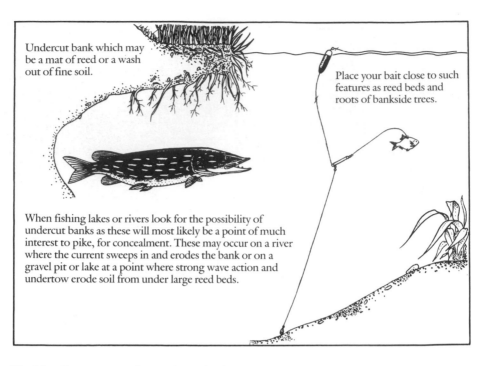

Undercut bank which may be a mat of reed or a wash out of fine soil.

Place your bait close to such features as reed beds and roots of bankside trees.

When fishing lakes or rivers look for the possibility of undercut banks as these will most likely be a point of much interest to pike, for concealment. These may occur on a river where the current sweeps in and erodes the bank or on a gravel pit or lake at a point where strong wave action and undertow erode soil from under large reed beds.

Fig 64   Paternoster swim (undercut bank).

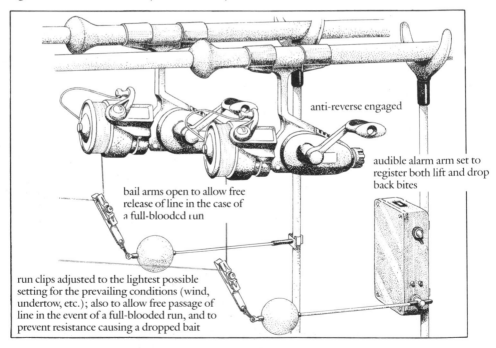

anti-reverse engaged

audible alarm arm set to register both lift and drop back bites

bail arms open to allow free release of line in the case of a full-blooded run

run clips adjusted to the lightest possible setting for the prevailing conditions (wind, undertow, etc.); also to allow free passage of line in the event of a full-blooded run, and to prevent resistance causing a dropped bait

Fig 65   Bite indicators (drop arm and audible).

Broadland tidal river 19lb 14oz fish for Chris Turnbull.

small amounts of movement and allow prompt action to set the hooks before the bait is swallowed. In many cases, the audible indicator only bleeps one short, sharp bleep to indicate the initial strike of the pike, followed some seconds later by a more sustained note as the bait is dealt with. In either case you should take the necessary action to set the hooks immediately.

With live- and deadbaits, positive bite indication is very important.

Once positioned, tighten down between rod and float to ensure that the line is sunken and straight to the bait. Slacken off to allow the float to come up to the vertical. Then tighten gently until the line lifts off the water at the rod tip, and attach your indicator. Pull it down to point B, as shown, then let it go. If it is tight enough, the indicator will rise slightly. If not, tighten up a little until it stays in position A.

Tight line will ensure that the bait cannot tangle with the reel line behind the float.

Fig 66   Setting bite indicators.

To ensure accuracy and that the bait presentation is correct, cast as illustrated with gentle overhead action for a short distance, and with a firm cast for greater distance. Align the rod directly over your head with the butt pointing at the exact spot your bait should land on. When the bait is airborne, follow up as shown in Fig 68.

Fig 67   Casting a livebait.

With bait in flight, lift your reel hand up and trap the running line between your finger and thumb just by the butt ring, still allowing the line free passage (point A). As the bait starts to fall to the water, squeeze down on the line and stop its passage. Then give a firm downwards pull (point B) to stop the flight of the bait and allow it to fall gently into the water. This will ensure that live- or injected baits are less likely to be damaged. You can also check the distance of the cast in this way when fishing near snags or obstacles.

Fig 68   Feathering the cast.

LEGERED LIVEBAIT

The last method of livebait fishing, legered livebait, involves the same sort of rigs as those seen in Fig 47. The only difference in use is the way the bait is mounted on the trace. All other information is the same. You need to mount the bait in a similar fashion to the river-rigged free-roving bait, with the upper trace treble through the lip and the end hook in the flank in front of and below the pelvic fins.

The most likely place to use this rig will be on large waters where you are unable to present a livebait on conventional float tackle at the distance at which the pike are feeding, either because of bankside activity, fishing pressure or simply because the fry are in a particular area. A typical example is given in Fig 36, which shows a reservoir fishery where fish lie between sixty and a hundred yards off

from the bank during the daytime due to pressure of angling and fry activity. Other likely places will be around islands or the far bank, if inaccessible on smaller lakes.

When casting these rigs with mounted livebaits, care should be taken in the cast not to rip the bait off. To reduce impact damage at the end of the cast, the line should be slowed down or feathered by trapping it between the forefinger and thumb just before the bait hits the water. This will allow the bomb and bait to enter the water with less impact – Fig 68 illustrates how and where to feather the line. It is worth the effort of practising this method to ensure your baits survive the cast and continue to act as livebaits.

Remember that livebaits are *not* obligatory and not the *only* method to catch pike – give the whole range of methods a try as they all have their applications.

Steve Aley with a fine lure-caught 18lb fish taken during the T.G. Lure Championships.

The biggest fish, 24¼lb, taken during the T.G. Lure Championship '88.

8 Lure Fishing

TACKLE

Tackle for lure fishing will be very similar in specification to your normal pike tackle. The only point to remember is that you will be casting relatively light weights over fairly short distances and it is very likely you will make contact with your quarry at very close range, perhaps even right under the rod tip.

The obvious type of rod to use will be of soft, compound-type action with a test curve of around two pounds. This will allow good casting and it will be a pleasure to hook and play the fish at close quarters on it. The reel you normally use, with the regular line of twelve pounds or so, will be sufficient to allow you to fish safely. If you choose to fish near snags, then go up to fifteen pounds or so.

Ideally, use a trace made from your regular wire, of around fifteen to twenty pounds, with a good swivel at either end. On the end that you will attach your lure you will require a good quick release link of the type shown in Fig 17. These styles of link are sound and under normal circumstances will withstand the rigours of lure fishing. When you use a spinner, the trace will require some additional attention as there is a strong chance that some twisting of the reel line will occur. Most normal swivels cannot cope with the high speed of spinning when they are under load, particularly when fishing in fast flowing rivers.

There are two very effective means of reducing line twist. One is to use a BB ball-bearing swivel which has its origins in game fishing, and is designed specifically to cope with the rigours of spinning with a Devon Minnow for salmon in some powerful rivers like the Wye. These swivels are available from good tackle dealers who have interests in game fishing. The second item, the anti-kink vane, is used by most lure anglers as it is more readily available (*see* Fig 18). The diagram shows how to set the anti-kink vane on to your reel line and how to mount your trace. Note the BB ball-bearing swivel which is at the head of the trace next to the vane. Another swivel is used at the spinner end of the trace to which the quick release snap link is fitted – this permits a secure fixing for the trace, but still allows maximum flexibility during casting and playing hooked fish.

There is no reason why you should not use an anti-kink vane when presenting plugs or spoons, in fact it may allow you more flexibility as you can swap from method to

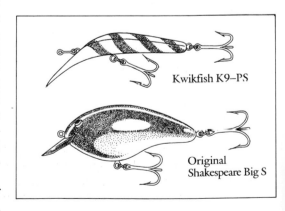

Kwikfish K9–PS

Original
Shakespeare Big S

Fig 69   Floating and slow-sinking plugs.

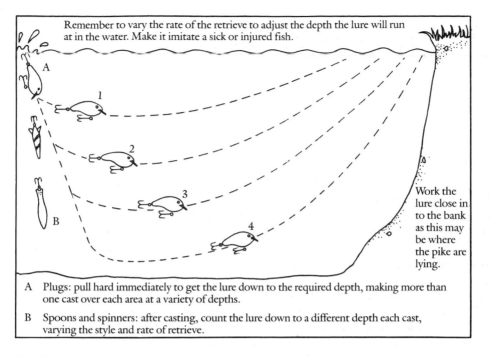

Fig 70   Action of plugs, spoons and spinners.

method at will and never have to worry about line twist! Generally, though, if you wish to use spoons and plugs predominantly then the trace shown in Fig 18 is still ideal, as all you have to do is leave off the anti-kink vane. If you should wish to use a spinner for a short period you will have no major problem, providing you took the advice given previously and fitted a ball-bearing swivel to your lure trace. Remember this advice and you will have ensured that your lure fishing will be much more enjoyable.

LURES

The question of what type of lures to carry is one that requires some thought as there are so many different types of spoons, plugs and spinners available to the angler. As with floats, they can be said to have hooked more anglers than fish! That is not to say that the

lures available are of no value, but it is better to make a start with some proven pike catchers and get some fish on the bank before moving on, once you are *hooked*, to experiment with the more varied range of lures available.

Plugs

Taking the bull by the horns and recommending which lures you should purchase and try, we need to classify each category and identify some models within it. Starting with plugs, there are two types you will require. One is a floating and diving plug – the most reliable and proven catcher is the original Shakespeare Big S (*see* Fig 69). This comes in several sizes, and the medium and larger sizes will provide a good casting range. It has an enticing wiggle on the retrieve and the depth of dive can be controlled by the retrieve rate. Use a fast retrieve for deep diving. A slow steady retrieve will maintain a depth set by an initial

A pristine 22lb tidal river pike for John Sadd.

Colin Brett with lure-caught small-water 17½lb pike.

quick pull, followed by the occasional quick pull and stop of the retrieve which will make the plug dive and rise in the water (*see* Fig 70).

The second type of plug is the slow sinker which will allow you to decide the depth you wish to fish by counting down the depth in seconds – taking an example of one second per foot, ten seconds would see the plug fishing at approximately ten feet. This type, the Kwikfish, and its action on the retrieve, is shown in Fig 69. This lure can be very useful in sizes from model K9 up to K12 (two and three-quarter to three and three-quarter inches respectively). It requires a very slow, hesitant style of retrieve as it has a very attractive wiggle.

Spoons

There are also two styles of spoon which are popular: the bar spoon, which is relatively long and thin with a shallow curve, and the short, wide spoon, with a fairly deep curve to make it flutter during its fall after casting and wobble during the retrieve. Fig 71 shows probably the most successful bar spoon available on the market, the ABU Toby and it is well worth holding this lure in sizes from five-eighths of an ounce to one ounce in silver, copper and brass metals. A newcomer to this particular category is a lure from Finland, the Kuusamo Professor, which is proving very effective and running a good second to the Toby. Size and material range for this lure are the same as the Toby.

The second style of spoon is often called the Norwich Spoon and it has a shorter, wider body which imparts a wobbling action to the retrieve. It will usually be used in shallower water than the heavy bar spoons. By virtue of its dual convex/concave shape it will

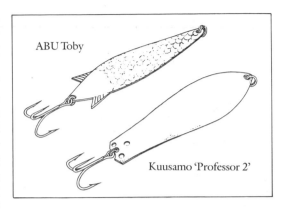

Fig 71   Spoons.

sink slowly in a fluttering action – a very useful spoon for use in shallow water and over weed, as may be found in places like the Norfolk Broads.

Spinners

The final kind of lure we need to carry is the spinner. This again is a relatively slow sinking lure which can be counted down to depth. The sort of spinners that you would be well advised to try are those manufactured by ABU and Mepps – in particular, models like ABU Droppen and Mepps Aglia. As with all lures, do not just cast and retrieve at the same place religiously, rather vary the way you retrieve, alternating between fast and slow. Twitch the tip up and down, and from side to side, or stop intermittently to put some life into the lure, be it plug, spoon or spinner. In running water allow the lure to flutter downstream in the current, then retrieve, stop, let it fall back in the current again and so on. Do not just chuck it in and pull it out – work it and you will catch and become hooked yourself.

9 Long-Range Fishing

The increased interest in pike fishing has led to a constant change and development of techniques to further increase our chance of capturing more and better fish. These technique developments have also changed pike fishing in other ways – they have given us more fish on the bank, but they have also educated our quarry on the harder fished waters in to moving out of range, even for the best casting angler. Whilst certain days will see the pike so preoccupied with feeding that they will forget their lessons and become accessible for a brief period, they will soon learn and return to a safer area.

To overcome this problem, determined anglers have evolved new methods through trial and error. These methods are long-range fishing with a static live- or deadbait, or long-

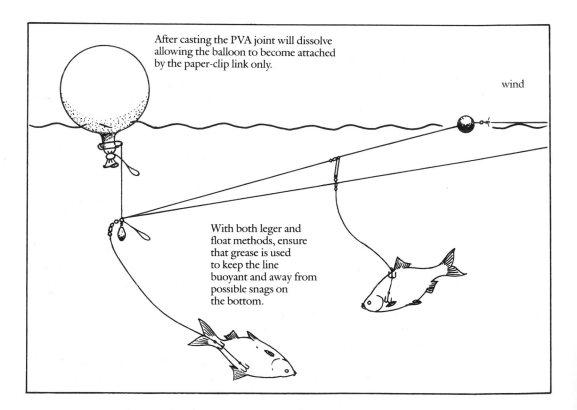

After casting the PVA joint will dissolve allowing the balloon to become attached by the paper-clip link only.

wind

With both leger and float methods, ensure that grease is used to keep the line buoyant and away from possible snags on the bottom.

Fig 72 Ballooning rig for live- and deadbaits.

range mobile drifting of live- or deadbaits. Both methods are producing fish from previously unfishable areas.

BALLOONING

A lot of thought went into ways of getting baits out to distances of up to 200 yards. The first method that became successful was ballooning. Fig 72 shows the rig to use to effect this. Basically, the idea is to suspend the live- or deadbait below a balloon and allow the wind to tow it across to the chosen area. You then strike the balloon off, depositing your bait and tackle exactly where you want it.

The rig shown overcomes some of the early problems of getting the balloon into the wind. It is often necessary to cast some distance to get into the wind, and in doing so it was common for the balloon to break free, necessitating total re-rigging only to suffer the same fate. The addition of the PVA fixed loop allowed a cast to be made safely, with the PVA tape dissolving a few minutes after settling in the water. The idea works with both bottom fished and paternostered (illustrated) baits, live or dead.

DRIFTING

Drifting a mobile bait will allow the angler to fish at ranges of up to 200 yards, and to fish more than one spot. You can actually search large areas of water until you locate your quarry. To go about fishing by this method you will require a float of the type shown in Fig 74 – commercially made versions of this float and similar designs are available from tackle dealers throughout the country. Drift fishing is relatively easy to do once you understand some very important points. Many of these are often overlooked with disappoint-

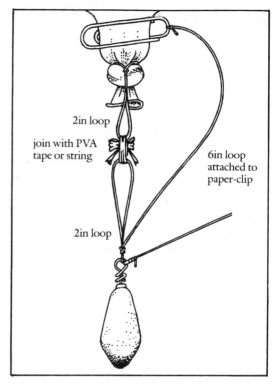

Fig 73 Ballooning casting link.

2in loop

join with PVA tape or string

6in loop attached to paper-clip

2in loop

ment for the angler and the pike – the angler does not catch, and if he does, the fish may be deeply hooked, causing the obvious problems.

To drift in deep or shallow water requires a float capable of supporting and pulling the bait, and of giving visibility at long range. The float illustrated meets these criteria. It also needs to be as trouble-free as possible. The float will often spin in variable winds, winding line around itself. It must be made to remain stable and upright in the strongest wind, but offer lifted bite registration by lying flat when this happens. It must also support the line at the extreme range fished – if it does not the line will sink, even if it is greased, due to its weight. Again, all these points are met by the illustrated float system. The bottom-only mounting of the float on a

A nice lure-caught double for Rob Hales during the T.G. Lure Championship '88.

Bottom only attached drift float showing the buoyancy aid supporting the line.

A day when all went to plan; 25¼lb and 27½lb trout-water pike taken on the drift.

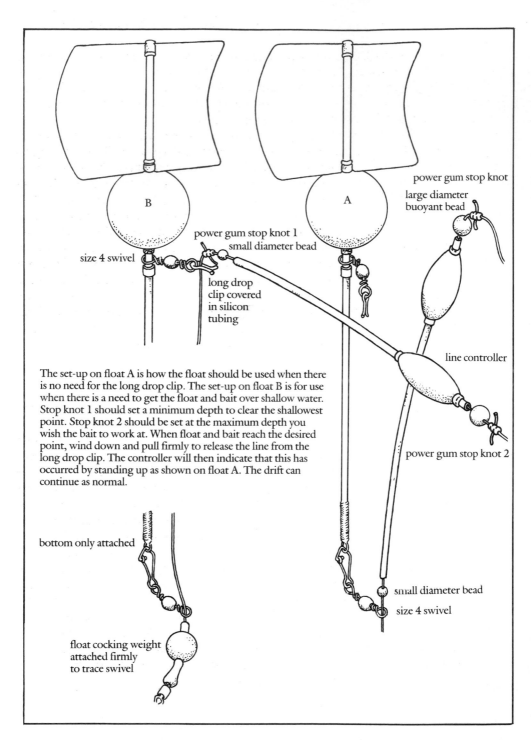

power gum stop knot

large diameter
buoyant bead

B

A

power gum stop knot 1
small diameter bead

size 4 swivel

long drop
clip covered
in silicon
tubing

line controller

The set-up on float A is how the float should be used when there
is no need for the long drop clip. The set-up on float B is for use
when there is a need to get the float and bait over shallow water.
Stop knot 1 should set a minimum depth to clear the shallowest
point. Stop knot 2 should be set at the maximum depth you
wish the bait to work at. When float and bait reach the desired
point, wind down and pull firmly to release the line from the
long drop clip. The controller will then indicate that this has
occurred by standing up as shown on float A. The drift can
continue as normal.

power gum stop knot 2

bottom only attached

small diameter bead

size 4 swivel

float cocking weight
attached firmly
to trace swivel

Fig 74   Super-controlled drifting float rigs.

swivel and a swivel-mounted long drop clip will allow the float to spin without fear of it tangling the line. Floats fixed top *and* bottom risk tangling.

The bite registration and float stability are controlled by the cocking weight firmly attached to the trace. The float has a long stem for leverage and is fully buoyant so it will instantly lie flat on the surface when the bait is raised by a striking fish, when it comes up to take it. The line is supported by the controller behind the float – even if you wind down and pull the float under and back fifty yards to redrift, the controller will pull the line back up clear of the surface. Top clips and body-mounted clips will detach during this manoeuvre and subsequently allow the line to sink, requiring a full retrieval to remedy. The illustrated float can be worked back and forth repeatedly until a pike takes. The controller also serves to hold the line clear of the float when it spins.

The bottom-only fixing of the float also gives good hooking qualities as it does not generate resistance when you strike, as does a waggler, rather it follows through on the strike. Top and body attached floats behave a bit like a stick float and absorb all the energy required to set the hooks.

You may wonder how you should strike at this extreme range. The answer is you do not – there is no point even trying. Immediately you get any indication of a take, by the float disappearing completely or lying flat on the surface, close the bail arm and start winding hard and fast to take up all the slack line between rod and float. This may take in twenty to thirty yards of slack and stretch in the line. Keep going until you feel some resistance building up, then give a firm sideways pull

until you feel the fish. This will have taken ten or maybe fifteen seconds from when the pike took your bait so do not hesitate. When you get some positive indication of a take, take the necessary action.

There are sometimes snags, shallows or bars in front of deep water. To set the rig to fish deep but not snag these obstacles, use the second layout of the rig shown in Fig 74. This incorporates a long drop clip system to allow you to set a primary and secondary depth. Cast as normal with everything set at the shallow setting, then, once you are out over the deeper water, tighten up to the float and effect a sharp pull to release the line from the long drop clip. The rig then sets itself to the deeper setting. The controller gives a visual indication of this as it goes from lying flat to standing upright – simple!

For long-range fishing, a twelve-foot rod in carbon fibre is probably the best for line control. A strong, fixed spool reel like the original Mitchell 300/410 with alloy spools is also recommended, as stretched nylon line puts terrific stress on spools and plastic ones will explode under the pressure! Plenty of line grease – Mucilin is a brand that works very well – should be applied to the line on the spool regularly throughout the drift, and for long-range static fishing, to keep the line clear of snags. With static bait fishing use a good, reliable drop arm indicator to tell you exactly the moment a bait is taken. Remember it may be some time before you actually set the hooks on the pike after it takes your bait.

Follow these guidelines and long-range fishing will be productive, giving you great pleasure and offering some consideration for the pike.

10 *Handling*

Handling and unhooking a captured fish is probably the most difficult area that you as a possible newcomer to pike fishing will encounter. Misunderstanding, handed down father to son over many years, has led many anglers to have an ill-formed view and deep-rooted fear of the pike as a species – and because of this the poor pike has had to suffer some pretty brutal treatment. From the advice given in this chapter you will see that it is possible to handle the fish you catch confidently and return them to the water unharmed.

Let's begin by clearing your mind of all the ideas you have been told of how a pike should be handled, based on those ill-formed stories that the pike is a vicious, man-eating creature. With a clear mind and will to succeed, the main point to remember is that you are the intelligent half of the pike/human duo and as such you must approach the task of landing, handling and hook removal with calm, control and confidence.

Good handling really begins with the way you put the hooks into your bait, but assum-

Having positioned your bait and set your indicator, stay close by and watch the activities for one of the detailed indications, then act swiftly to set the hooks.

Fig 75 Indicator actions – the take!

Even the smallest pike deserves respect and good handling.

ing you have heeded the advice in the appropriate chapters, your next move will be when the run or bite actually comes. If you are using drop arm indicators and these register a bite, do not hesitate or wait for something to happen. Get to your rod, take it from the rests, close your bail arm, or tighten the drag if you are using the newer free-running reels, and if no line is being taken, tighten down gently and feel if there is any activity at the other end. If there is no noticeable activity you will feel the resistance if you tighten some more and gently pull the rod upwards – Fig 76 shows the activities at this point. If you are unsure, wind down to tighten up the line fully, and make a firm sideways sweep to set the hooks – something took the trouble to move the indicator and even if you do not connect with the pike you will not risk a deep hooking. Experience has proven that some

takes give no more than a simple jerk on the indicator, causing a single bleep on an audible indicator that is sensitive enough. A strike made after just this minor indication lands nine out of ten fish.

LANDING THE FISH

Having successfully hooked your pike you should keep a firm pressure on your fish. To keep control, apply the necessary side strain to turn the fish away from any snags, and gently tire the fish in open water, taking care not to play the fish for an excessive time (*see* Fig 79). Once brought to the net, upon seeing you, the fish will endeavour to escape.

It is at this point that you should be alert to the pike's actions and have your large landing net – at least a thirty-inch, long-arm triangu-

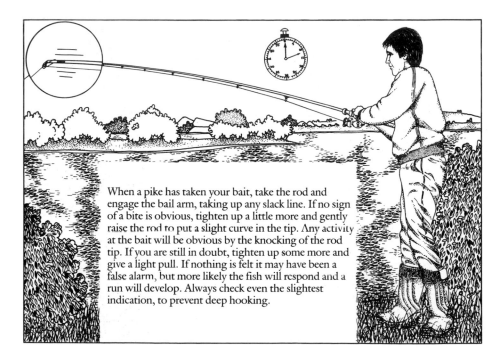

When a pike has taken your bait, take the rod and engage the bail arm, taking up any slack line. If no sign of a bite is obvious, tighten up a little more and gently raise the rod to put a slight curve in the tip. Any activity at the bait will be obvious by the knocking of the rod tip. If you are still in doubt, tighten up some more and give a light pull. If nothing is felt it may have been a false alarm, but more likely the fish will respond and a run will develop. Always check even the slightest indication, to prevent deep hooking.

Fig 76 Feeling for activity at the bait.

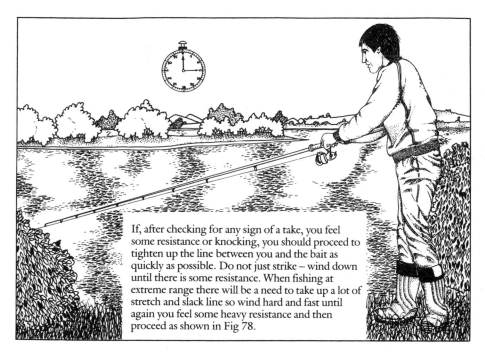

If, after checking for any sign of a take, you feel some resistance or knocking, you should proceed to tighten up the line between you and the bait as quickly as possible. Do not just strike – wind down until there is some resistance. When fishing at extreme range there will be a need to take up a lot of stretch and slack line so wind hard and fast until again you feel some heavy resistance and then proceed as shown in Fig 78.

Fig 77   Winding down to make contact.

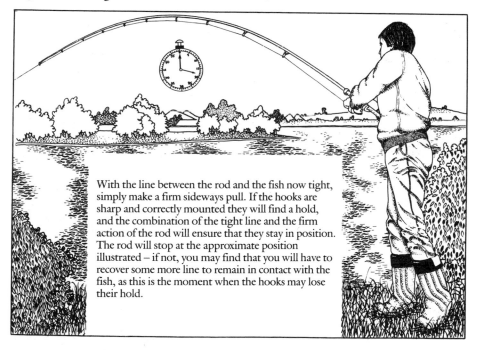

With the line between the rod and the fish now tight, simply make a firm sideways pull. If the hooks are sharp and correctly mounted they will find a hold, and the combination of the tight line and the firm action of the rod will ensure that they stay in position. The rod will stop at the approximate position illustrated – if not, you may find that you will have to recover some more line to remain in contact with the fish, as this is the moment when the hooks may lose their hold.

Fig 78   Give a firm, sideways pull to set the hooks.

The fish will endeavour to get to whatever snags there are. You can only attempt to stop it by applying side strain in the opposite direction to which it wishes to go. The pressure will usually tire the fish, or turn it.

When the fish is near the bank, keep a low profile and continue to apply some pressure to tire the fish. If it spots you it will continue to fight hard and on a short line may exert enough pressure to find a weakness in a trace or your reel line. Do not startle the fish or tire it for a long time.

Fig 79   Apply side strain to stop, turn and tire the fish for landing.

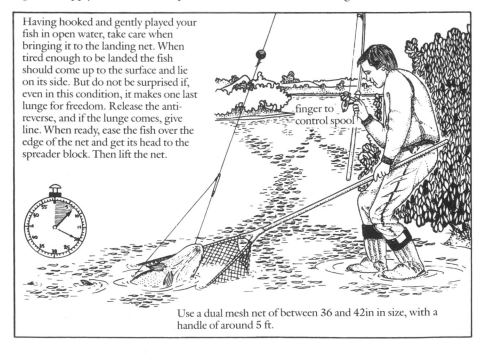

Having hooked and gently played your fish in open water, take care when bringing it to the landing net. When tired enough to be landed the fish should come up to the surface and lie on its side. But do not be surprised if, even in this condition, it makes one last lunge for freedom. Release the anti-reverse, and if the lunge comes, give line. When ready, ease the fish over the edge of the net and get its head to the spreader block. Then lift the net.

finger to control spool

Use a dual mesh net of between 36 and 42in in size, with a handle of around 5 ft.

Fig 80   Landing hooked fish.

With the fish on the unhooking mat, lay the restraining flap over it and kneel on either side, holding it secure. Insert your hand under the gill cover and run your fingers up to the front of the jaw. Pull the jaw upwards to open the mouth. Make sure you know where the hooks are before you put your hand under the gill cover.

With smaller fish or for a better access to the hooks, it may be necessary to stand up to unhook the fish. Keep the same hand-hold and slowly stand up, picking up the fish from a crouched position. If a friend is with you, get him to hold the wrist of the tail to stop the fish from wriggling and injuring itself or your hand.

Make sure you take the fish to soft ground and then use a soft pad or unhooking mat to protect the fish.

Fig 81   Unhooking on a handling mat.

lar net – ready submerged in the water. If you have gently tired your fish it should readily come into the margins or to the boat on its side, with its head raised by the pull of your line. It should then be eased over the draw cord, as shown in Fig 80, until its head reaches the spreader block at the handle, at which point the net should be raised to engulf the fish. Do not, under any circumstances, consider using a small landing net and *never* use a gaff – these will result in more pike suffering and eventually dying.

Having netted your pike, now lift the net and gently move the fish to a grassy bank, if available, on to a wet sack or a proper handling mat, as shown in Fig 81. On gravel pits, reservoirs with hard banks or in a boat, use the same idea – a wet sack or foam carpet underlay laid out well in advance. A pike can suffer serious damage if it is allowed to thrash or writhe around on loose gravel, stones or on the boards in the bottom of your boat.

UNHOOKING

Once the fish is on the handling mat or sack, cover it with a second piece of wet material, or the special flap on the handling mat, then kneel down with one leg on each side of the fish, firmly holding it between your legs. Then turn the fish on to its back, so that it is ready for unhooking. It is now that you will need to apply a very confident approach to your handling.

Some pike anglers advocate using a glove for this next part of hook removal, but the best approach is to work without gloves as they can catch on the gill rakers and cause unseen damage. The glove is supposed to protect the angler's hand from the sharp edges of the gill raker, but in fact all they do is mask damage that is occurring when you do it wrong! It is far better to scratch your hand and take more care than to push on wrongly, unaware you are causing damage.

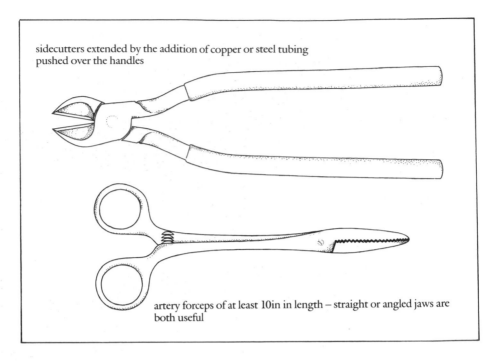

sidecutters extended by the addition of copper or steel tubing pushed over the handles

artery forceps of at least 10in in length – straight or angled jaws are both useful

Fig 82   Forceps and extended sidecutters.

Having positioned the fish, take a pair of long forceps at least twelve inches long, either straight or with angled jaws (*see* Fig 82). With the other hand slide your fingers under the gill cover, gently lift it and proceed to slide your fingers up to the centre point between both covers under the chin, as shown in Fig 83. Remember to take extreme care not to catch your hand in the gill filaments or on the gill rakers – if you break or damage them the pike could slowly bleed to death.

Once in position, gently pull the lower jaw towards you and eventually the weight of the pike will cause the mouth to open. If it does not, gently push the upper jaw away from the lower jaw until the mouth is open. If you are alone and are unable to keep the mouth open, you may have to use a gag. If you do then make sure it has the ends bound in elastic tape to cover the sharp points, or use one similar to that illustrated in Fig 83, but do try and work without a gag where possible.

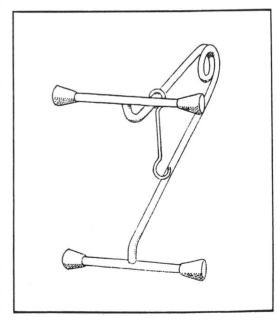

Fig 83   Modified gag.

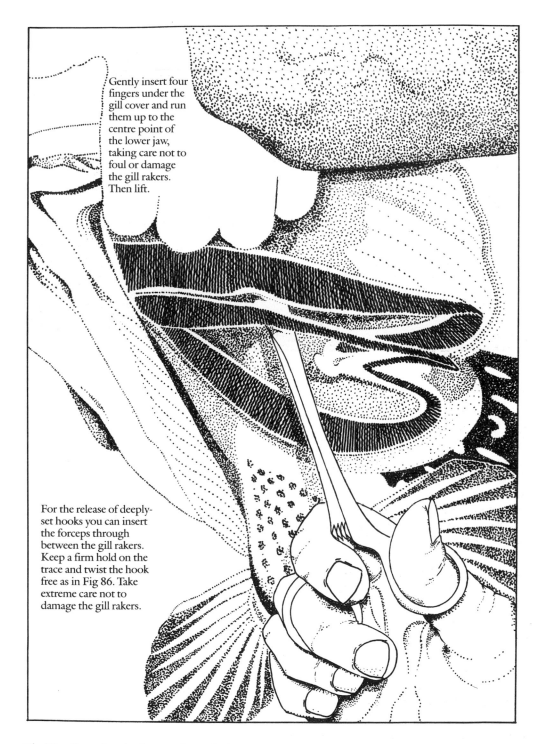

Gently insert four fingers under the gill cover and run them up to the centre point of the lower jaw, taking care not to foul or damage the gill rakers. Then lift.

For the release of deeply-set hooks you can insert the forceps through between the gill rakers. Keep a firm hold on the trace and twist the hook free as in Fig 86. Take extreme care not to damage the gill rakers.

Fig 84 Inserting the forceps through the gillrakers.

Richard Howard supports a prize Ardingley Reservoir 25lb 5oz pike.

If you are without a gag you can use an alternative method which involves standing up and lifting the pike by the jaw with your hand again under the gill cover. The weight of the fish will ensure the mouth stays open. Big fish are usually no trouble, but the smaller ones sometimes do not have enough body weight to keep their mouths open. However, perseverance will see you succeed. On each illustration of handling techniques there is a clock face indicating how long each activity should take. Bear these in mind and remember that the shorter the time you have your fish out of the water, the better.

Now that the mouth is open, if your timing of the strike was right and you used a recommended hooking layout to suit your bait size, you will find your hooks are visible in the mouth. They will probably be in the scissors, the corner of the mouth, and you should find their removal is no problem. Hold the trace tight, either in your teeth if you are alone, or

get a friend or nearby angler to pull it tight if possible, then gently unhook. Release the nearer up-trace hook first, then the lower end hook, and carefully pull the trace clear, leaving the forceps attached to the hook.

If the end hook is out of sight, because the fish has turned and swallowed the bait, possibly your hook layout was incorrect for the bait size or you delayed in striking. Whatever the cause, there is no need to panic. If you have followed the advice in previous chapters and have been using semi-barbless hooks then even deeply hooked fish can be unhooked with care. You must again concentrate and act calmly. Proceed exactly as before up to opening the mouth.

Once you have located the hooks, by pulling on the trace until the upper hook is visible, this time carefully get a companion to pull firmly on the trace to keep the hook visible. Then you must insert the forceps through between the gills and rakers (*see* Fig 84),

Chris Turnbull with a Broadland tidal river fish carefully laid out on padding for protection.

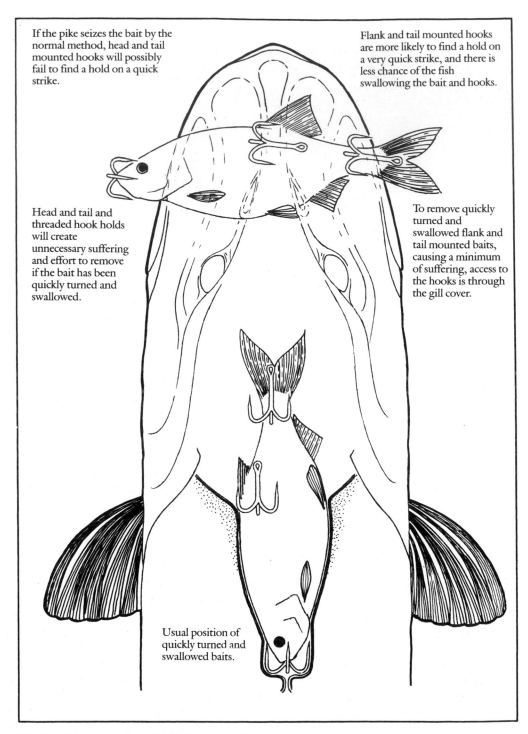

If the pike seizes the bait by the normal method, head and tail mounted hooks will possibly fail to find a hold on a quick strike.

Flank and tail mounted hooks are more likely to find a hold on a very quick strike, and there is less chance of the fish swallowing the bait and hooks.

Head and tail and threaded hook holds will create unnecessary suffering and effort to remove if the bait has been quickly turned and swallowed.

To remove quickly turned and swallowed flank and tail mounted baits, causing a minimum of suffering, access to the hooks is through the gill cover.

Usual position of quickly turned and swallowed baits.

Fig 85   The positions of deadbait during the take.

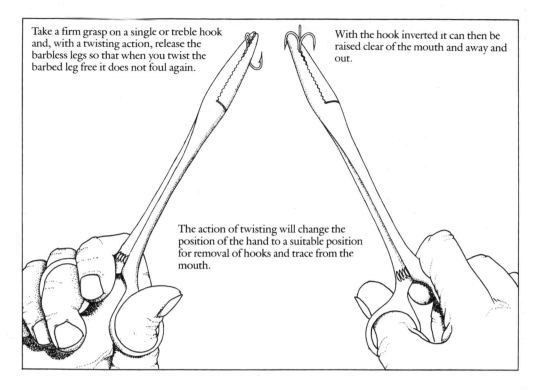

Take a firm grasp on a single or treble hook and, with a twisting action, release the barbless legs so that when you twist the barbed leg free it does not foul again.

With the hook inverted it can then be raised clear of the mouth and away and out.

The action of twisting will change the position of the hand to a suitable position for removal of hooks and trace from the mouth.

Fig 86   Turning hooks free.

clamp the forceps to the shank of the hook, and gently twist the hook to release each point in turn. This is when barbless hooks become a more obvious advantage. Get the person holding the trace to pull firmly but gently until the other hook comes into sight. The throat tissue will probably start to come out into the mouth, but do not worry or panic. Gently repeat as before, releasing the hook and gently taking the trace out of the pike's mouth, then withdraw the forceps through the gills. If you cannot release the barb you can cut the shank at the bend with an extended pair of sidecutters as shown in Fig 82. This is a last resort, but it is better than leaving the hooks in, sealing the throat and committing the pike to death by starvation. Confidence and care will ensure that

you have the pleasure of seeing your pike survive. But remember, prevention of deep hooking is better than the cure.

THE RELEASE

When you have successfully unhooked your pike and seen just how simple it can be, you should slip it back into the landing net and drop it back into the water to recover from the unhooking, particularly if it has taken a few minutes. You will probably want to weigh your fish and maybe take a photograph, so whilst the fish recovers you should set everything out ready. You will have plenty of time, as the pike should be given fifteen to twenty minutes in the water before you proceed. Wet

109

Hard earned and carefully returned.

Gaff damage found on a River Bure double.

A Broadland 20lb fish is chin lifted into the boat.

the weigh sling and cover the ground with a wet sack or handling mat. When ready, lift the fish out of the water and carry it, in the net, to where you will complete the weighing. Then get your photographs taken with the fish as near to the ground as possible. When you are holding it for the photograph you can predict when the fish is likely to want to wriggle and thrash. Do not worry if you feel the fish tense up on your hands. Simply lower it to the mat and cover its head. Its flapping action is nothing more than its attempt to swim away, which obviously it cannot. If you allow it to flap you are likely to let it injure itself so cover and restrain it.

Do not hug the fish close to your body as the zips and buckles on most coats and suits will rip off some scales and render the fish

Place the fish in the thoroughly wetted weigh sling and quickly check the weight. The illustrated sling is very kind to all species. Return the fish to the water in the sling.

Fig 87   Weighing the fish.

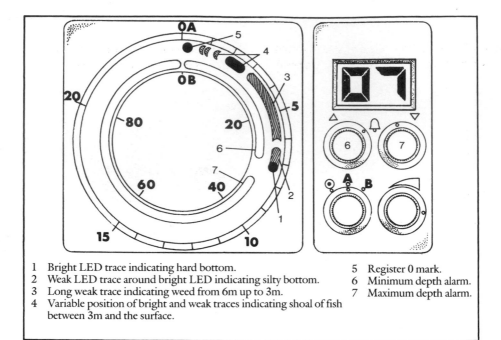

1 Bright LED trace indicating hard bottom.
2 Weak LED trace around bright LED indicating silty bottom.
3 Long weak trace indicating weed from 6m up to 3m.
4 Variable position of bright and weak traces indicating shoal of fish between 3m and the surface.
5 Register 0 mark.
6 Minimum depth alarm.
7 Maximum depth alarm.

Fig 88   Echo sounder and read-outs.

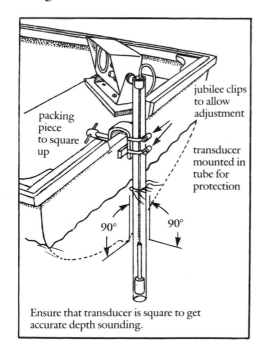

Ensure that transducer is square to get accurate depth sounding.

Fig 89   Transducer mountings.

vulnerable to fungus and disease. Just lay it gently down. When it is calm, quickly take your photographs and get the fish into the landing net or weigh sling and carry it back to the water. Do not carry it to the water in your hands, as if it decides to jump out of your grasp and land on the floor it will damage internal organs in the process and may subsequently die.

Once it is back in the water, gently support the fish until it is able to swim off. If the fish should turn on its side or go right over so its belly comes up, you *must* put it back up the right way and support it. Watch it until it can support itself – this may take thirty minutes, an hour or even longer, but if you care, you will see the task through. For longer retention and for holding a good fish until cameras are available you can use a large keep sack at least four feet wide by six feet deep, or one of the new pike tubes that are now available, but do try and refrain from holding fish unnecessarily. The finest feeling you can get is seeing returned fish swimming strongly away, healthy and none the worse for their experience – it's probably as good as actually hooking it.

11 *Boat Fishing*

Until recently the vast majority of pike anglers never had the need to consider boat fishing; instead the normal style would be to fish from the banks of lakes, pits or rivers. However, we have now reached a stage where waters such as Grafham and Rutland – both staunch trout waters – will open up for a few weekends at the end of each trout season to allow anglers to fish for the pike they hope are still there. A few big fish do still exist but not as many as we would like. However, record potential does exist despite the intensive netting programme, as Robert Wort's fly-caught, potential record fish proves.

There is now a progression towards the commercialisation of privately-managed trout waters, in order to make money all the year round. This means that the average pike angler has been able to pursue his sport afloat, although many have been disappointed. This disappointment is due mainly to inexperience, and the fact that there is very little help available to guide the angler round the difficulties that exist in boat fishing. This chapter aims to make some suggestions and outline some basic facts on safety and boat lore, although much will depend on whether you just hire your boat on each visit to the chosen venue, or whether you wish ultimately to purchase your own boat.

CHOOSING A BOAT

The ideal boat for pike fishing will differ from angler to angler, but if you follow a basic guideline the purchase of a good boat will turn out to be an investment. The wrong choice will lumber you with a liability. The optimum size of a boat for two people will be a length of twelve to fourteen feet, with a width (or beam) of five feet. Whilst fishing alone can be very enjoyable, you are well advised to get together with a good friend and work as a team. A good friend is as important as a good boat because it can be pretty hard when the going gets tough in bad weather, and even harder when one of the two is getting all the fish – it does happen and it takes true friendship to keep it all together.

There are several considerations if you decide to fish alone, the first being whether you wish to be mobile and able to fish where and when you want. If you do, you will require a light and durable boat, an ideal example being a 10½-foot dinghy made in glass reinforced plastic (GRP) by Fibrocell. This comes with a large built-in buoyancy compartment – you will need the support of this in the event of a capsize or swamping. This size of boat allows good freedom of movement to a lone angler and at a push can take two. Most importantly, though, you will be able to launch and retrieve a lightweight dinghy like this from a trailer at any access point or slipway on your own. If you choose to use a boat at one venue only, then you are not restricted by size – if you can acquire a mooring and leave the boat on site you may have as big a boat as you wish. The only shortcoming will be when you feel the need to fish on a new river or lake.

15ft Shetland boat fully prepared for use as pike angler's work horse.

Alternatively, if you choose to team up with a good friend, any boat of sufficient size will be of use, but you will still require a boat that can easily be manhandled by two. A boat in GRP with simulated clinker effect, and twelve to fourteen feet long will give you a safe and stable platform to fish from – a good example is an Orkney Longliner. A boat of this size will be fairly easy to launch and retrieve at any convenient access point. Again, look for a dinghy with built-in buoyancy as it is much easier to capsize a boat with two anglers in it, than when there is only one.

Something many anglers learn the hard way is that all movement in a boat has to be co-ordinated and planned. Neither angler should move without advising the other – if both move to one end or side of the boat it will become unstable and list, and maybe even capsize. Remember to move in a planned way,

Good oars, sleeves and matching rowlocks ensure good and quiet rowing.

and locate your tackle and equipment evenly in the boat so as not to clutter the free movement of both anglers and affect the boat's stability. Take something to bail the boat with in the event of heavy rain or leaking due to damage. You will also find a good-sized bailer handy when the call of nature comes – it is far safer to relieve yourself into the bailer, than resist or lean over the edge of your boat, particularly if your companion decides to move without warning you first.

HIRING A BOAT

Your choice of boat should be related to the water you wish to use it on – a big water will ultimately require a big, stable boat not a small, unstable one. You can still use your larger boat on your smaller venue, of course.

However, you may choose to hire at your given venue which will, in many cases, be a trout fishery. Whilst the boats will be good work boats, they are rarely designed for pike fishing, and generally have only a very small smooth flat surface area to lay out a big pike for unhooking, should you be successful in catching one. Those who do rely on hire boats should take note of the advice given for customising a boat and be prepared to take along with them items necessary to make the boat usable. Thrashing around in the bottom of a boat will cause descaling and ultimately death for a big pike.

Whether your own or a hired boat is to be used, make sure you own or obtain from the hirer a buoyancy aid – it is your choice whether you wear one, but anybody who goes afloat in the depths of winter is running a great risk, which is even greater if he does not wear a life-jacket or buoyancy aid. These will be available at all the commercially-operated trout fisheries where boats are for hire, so do ask.

ADDITIONAL EQUIPMENT

Whatever type of boat you choose, you will need to have some basic items to transform it into an acceptable working area. For personal comfort you will need a good foam cushion, covered and sealed to be waterproof, as eight hours or more sitting in a boat does nasty things to your nether regions. For the welfare of the pike, you should obtain a large piece of foam carpet underlay, approximately 6 × 6 ft or bigger if possible, to cushion the movements of your fish during unhooking. You can carry, in addition to this, a square of plastic tarpaulin of about 5 × 5 ft, to lay on the foam. This prevents water from the foam soaking your legs when kneeling on it, and doubles as a protective cover for your tackle in times of inclement weather. Finally, to further aid unhooking, you can also use an ET-style unhooking mat to fully control the pike and prevent further chance of damage. You may feel that all this is a bit excessive, but you should consider it the least you should carry to save damaging a pike.

Ropes

Whilst most boats hired to you will have mud weights or anchors with ropes attached, it is always worth carrying a set of your own ropes to avoid disappointment. There is nothing worse than locating a hot spot in twenty to thirty feet of water only to find you cannot fish it properly when the boat drifts uncontrollably because the ropes are too short or the weights too light! The best suggestion is not to use the cheap polypropylene-type rope, as this is difficult to knot and very hard on cold wet hands when pulling up the anchor. It is better to pay a visit to a good chandlery and get a rope at least three-eighths of an inch in diameter – the extra price is a very good investment. A good mud weight made of concrete will weigh something around fourteen to twenty pounds, and can be cast in something like a bucket or large ice-cream container with a loop of galvanised or stainless wire set in deeply during the pouring of the concrete.

Rowlocks

Always carry a spare set of rowlocks. If you own your own boat, breakage may occur; if you are hiring, you will be able to replace theirs with your own if they are the conventional slide-in type. A lot of reservoirs are now using fixed point oars, which are very good. On shallow waters noisy oars and rowlocks will spook your fish before you get near them, so a good tight fit between oars and rowlocks and between rowlocks and the boat is important. A roll of PVC insulating tape is very useful for tightening up loose rowlocks. If it is your own boat, you should fit the nylon-type rowlocks and ensure they are replaced when they become loose on the oar. Make sure you also have a good set of oars and fit them with sleeves to ensure a good fit in the rowlock. Good chandlers will stock all the necessary items at reasonable prices.

Tackle

The amount of tackle you take with you in a boat needs some careful consideration as the room available is limited, and you need to be able to move freely and safely when playing, landing and subsequently handling the pike you will be hoping to catch. The normal tackle you take when fishing from the bank will include items you will not need, so these are the first things to remove from your boat tackle. Bite indicators, rod rests and umbrellas are items that immediately come to mind, but stow them in the car just in case you cannot get your boat out for one reason or another –

at least with these you can bank fish if necessary and save the day.

Hard body or tubular-type tackle boxes are the other major items you should not take into the boat. Firstly, they are inflexible and cannot be moved quietly or without a lot of hassle. The boat hull will act like a loudspeaker and amplify any noise. The sort of holdall you should consider is the rucksack-style holdall, as supplied by Trevor Moss, or the match bag marketed by Kevin Nash. Both hold all you will require and are reasonably waterproof. If two of you are fishing together, you need only use one holdall between you to save on space – a small bag can then be used to carry your flasks and food. Most of your regular items can be carried in the holdall – you should just decide what you normally carry and then work out what to leave behind. The tackle carried can be tidily stowed in two ice-cream containers or Tupperware boxes.

Echo Sounders

An echo sounder is probably the best investment you can make, particularly if you intend doing a lot of boat fishing. You will learn more about the water you are fishing in a couple of hours with a sounder than in a lifetime of fishing it. A new breed of sounder is now available, but only at some considerable cost, which is in fact well beyond the reach of most anglers' pockets. These hi-tech sounders are the Lowrance Eagle MkII and the Humminbird, both imported from the USA. They both use liquid crystal displays and actually identify the fish in colour! However, we can still obtain the necessary information from the more humble echo sounders like the Seafarer and the Nasa Marine, Stingray. The latter has dual liquid crystal display and light-emitting diode spinner read-outs and dual adjustable minimum and maximum

Mobility for the lone pike angler is a small dinghy and trailer. A Fibrocell 10½ft dinghy.

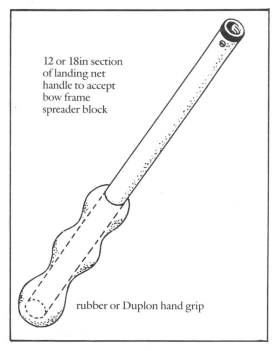

12 or 18in section of landing net handle to accept bow frame spreader block

rubber or Duplon hand grip

Fig 90   Short landing net handle.

depth audible alarms. The information available on the spinner dial will give you much help in reading what is going on below the boat once you have gained some experience. Fig 88 shows some typical displays and what they mean. If you decide to purchase an echo sounder, stick to the advice offered by the manufacturer on how to use and install it – particularly in the case of the transducer and its connecting lead, as these are made to a calculated measurement.

Landing Net

One item that will always be a point of discussion between boat anglers is the landing net. Some like to use just the arms and net and scoop the fish in – this works well enough but it leaves the angler draped over the edge of the boat holding the net. It is also very difficult to net a fish if you are alone. Others use the net in its normal form with a long handle. Again, this will suffice, but stowing a fully

Large waters and boats demand respect and a buoyancy aid.

Orkney longliner on Lough Oughter, County Cavan, Ireland.

Small 12in handle on a large capacity landing net. Use a 36 or 42in arm, bow frame type for easy knock down to handle fish in the boat.

Fig 91   Net in use.

made-up net is space-consuming. It may be helpful when fishing alone, but again it is cumbersome when two anglers are confined in a boat – try swinging round in a boat with a five-foot handle attached to your net, whilst holding on to the arms! Illustrated in Fig 90 is a short handle twelve inches long, with a good rubber grip fitted and standard 42-inch arm. This net takes up little space either folded down or assembled and stowed in the corner of the boat.

Transporting Bait

The transportation of bait supplies needs consideration, and with livebaits two options are available. One is an ET cage or similar; another option you can adopt is to carry a net. Ideal for the job is a small, round-pan landing net, taken off the frame. Slip this over your bait bucket – a three-gallon type is ideal – and secure it with a strong, wide elastic strap (*see* Fig 54). This is suspended over the side and secured with a strong cord. It will keep the bait fresh and will be easily usable. If you wish to use deadbaits, a good supply of frozen baits, smelt, herrings and naturals can be kept in good condition by storing in large frozen boily bags accompanied by a freezer pack. This ensures a tidy boat as well, because you only take out what you use.

METHODS

Methods of fishing from a boat will involve many of the regular tactics used from the bank. However, in deep water where a float is difficult to use you will need some alternative form of bite indication. This comes in the form of open bail arms and line clips as shown in Fig 92 (which also shows a boat rod rest, available from some good tackle shops, which is useful when space is required in a smallish boat). The other method of bite indication is to use clutches slackened off on rear drag,

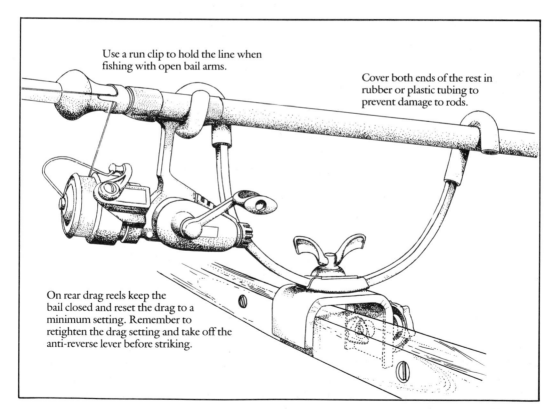

Use a run clip to hold the line when fishing with open bail arms.

Cover both ends of the rest in rubber or plastic tubing to prevent damage to rods.

On rear drag reels keep the bail closed and reset the drag to a minimum setting. Remember to retighten the drag setting and take off the anti-reverse lever before striking.

Fig 92   Boat rod rest, showing use of run clips.

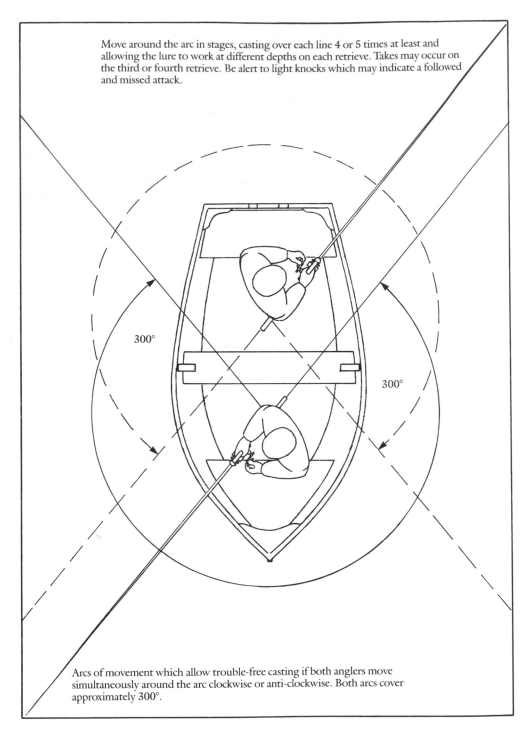

Move around the arc in stages, casting over each line 4 or 5 times at least and allowing the lure to work at different depths on each retrieve. Takes may occur on the third or fourth retrieve. Be alert to light knocks which may indicate a followed and missed attack.

300°

300°

Arcs of movement which allow trouble-free casting if both anglers move simultaneously around the arc clockwise or anti-clockwise. Both arcs cover approximately 300°.

Fig 93   Lure fishing sequence around a boat with two anglers.

Chris Turnbull with the catch of a lifetime – pike of 27lb 8oz and 23lb 14oz from a Broadland tidal river.

fixed spool reels, particularly the new Bait-runner reels from Shimano. On multiplier reels with free spool and ratchet engaged, a take is indicated by the ratchets ticking as line is pulled off the rotating spools.

Lure fishing from a boat allows two anglers to fish a very large area of water alternately around the boat (*see* Fig 93). Remember to work methodically round the arc and fish various depths along each line of cast until you have exhausted the possibility of covering a fish.

One very useful method of fishing from a boat is trolling or, as some call it, trailing a bait. This can be done on deep water, shallow water and in the moving waters of lowland rivers. The basic rig is shown in Fig 59, and is similar to a free-roving livebait rig. The

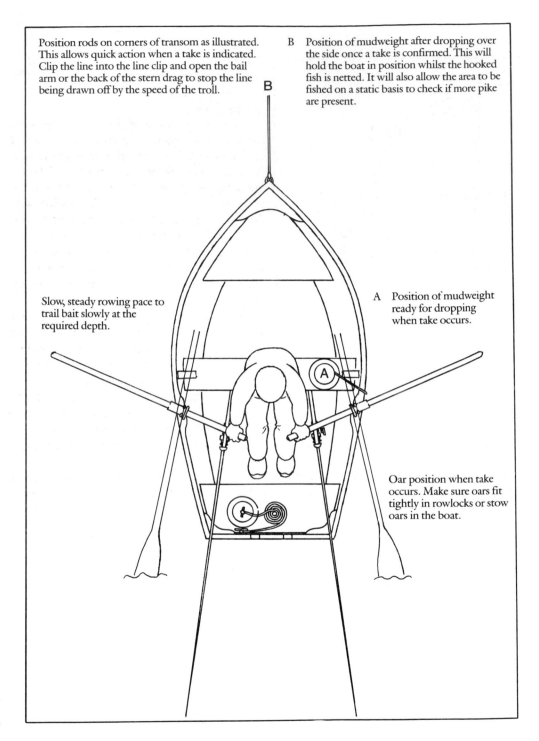

Position rods on corners of transom as illustrated. This allows quick action when a take is indicated. Clip the line into the line clip and open the bail arm or the back of the stern drag to stop the line being drawn off by the speed of the troll.

B Position of mudweight after dropping over the side once a take is confirmed. This will hold the boat in position whilst the hooked fish is netted. It will also allow the area to be fished on a static basis to check if more pike are present.

B

Slow, steady rowing pace to trail bait slowly at the required depth.

A Position of mudweight ready for dropping when take occurs.

A

Oar position when take occurs. Make sure oars fit tightly in rowlocks or stow oars in the boat.

Fig 94 Rod and mud weight positions when trolling.

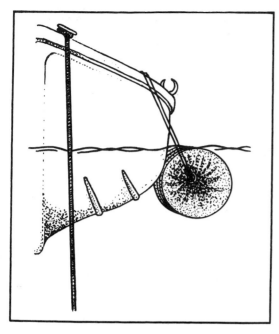

Fig 95 Pike tube in use on a boat.

difference is that the tackle is set slightly over depth, and, ideally, the float should be locked at the desired depth, as in some circumstances the float can work down the line and lift the bait too high. Fig 94 shows the rod position during trolling – this is important in that it helps your control when a take is indicated by line being pulled from the line clips or the ratchet tickings.

Note the position of the mud weight on the seat, ready so that when a take comes, it can be dropped over the side to stop the boat drifting away from the location. This is important as there can be more than one fish in the location of the first fish. With well-fitted oars and rowlocks it is possible to just let go and let them hang on the side of the boat; alternatively, pull them onboard or secure a cord to each oar and tie them to the seat or some other suitably secure point – they are no good if you lose them!

Deep water trolling requires a more complex approach and space is not available to give the method justice. The main point to remember with a trailed bait is not to take it too fast but rather proceed very slowly and quietly. If you know there is a bar, snag or change in depth you can raise the bait to clear it by momentarily speeding up the trail then slowing down when you clear it. This method will very likely produce a fish when static fished baits fail to do so. Set yourself up properly and give it a try, it is well worth the effort.

Further Reading

John Bailey and Martyn Page, *Pike, The Predator Becomes the Prey*, (The Crowood Press)

Fred Buller, *Pike and the Pike Angler*, (Stanley Paul)

Bill Chillingsworth, *Tactics for Big Pike*, (Beekay)

Neville Fickling, *Pike Fishing in the 80s*, (Beekay)

Barrie Rickards and Ken Whitehead, *Spinning and Plug Fishing*, (Boydell Press)

John Sidley, *River Piking*, (Boydell Press)

Tony Wheildon, *Fishing Skills – Pike Fishing*, (Ward Lock)

Index

INDEX